SIX-FIGURE
CONSULTING

SIX-FIGURE CONSULTING

How to Have
a Great
Second Career

Dr. Gary Scott Goodman

AMACOM
American Management Association

New York • Atlanta • Boston • Chicago • Kansas City • San Francisco • Washington, D. C.
Brussels • Mexico City • Tokyo • Toronto

This book is available at a special
discount when ordered in bulk quantities.
For information, contact Special Sales Department,
AMACOM, a division of American Management Association,
1601 Broadway, New York, NY 10019.

Library of Congress Cataloging-in-Publication Data

Goodman, Gary S.
    Six-Figure consulting : how to have a great second career / Gary
Scott Goodman.
        p.   cm.
    Includes bibliographical references and index.
    ISBN 0-8144-7958-8
    1. Business consultants—Vocational guidance—United States.
I. Title.
HD69.C6G657   1997
001'.028'73—DC21   97–2099
                                                             CIP

Printing number

10   9   8   7   6   5   4   3   2   1

To my wife,
colleague, and best friend,
Dr. Deanne Goodman,
and to our daughter, the wonderful
Amanda Leigh

Contents

Acknowledgments

I would like to thank Jessica Wainwright, my agent from the Literary Group International, and Mary Glenn, my editor at AMACOM Books, for their efforts to bring this book into the world.

I would also like to express my appreciation to my consulting clients, and to you, the reader.

SIX-FIGURE CONSULTING

1

The Consulting Lifestyle

*D*o you have trouble holding down a steady job? Do you get antsy after a year or two, and look forward to a new challenge?

Or do you shudder when you imagine spending the better part of your life with a single company or entity, reporting to the same bosses until they retire you to the farm?

You're not alone. And you're not crazy.

You might be a consultant, at least by temperament. Consulting might offer you a lifestyle that fits nicely with your disposition.

✳✳✳✳✳✳✳✳✳✳

Careers are a lot like the track and field events in the Olympics.

Some runners are super-quick in the sprints. Others don't show their prowess until they hit marathons. Sprinters and marathoners can both earn gold medals, but they have very different strengths.

They can seldom run each other's races as effectively as their own. You need to ask yourself what kind of runner you are when it comes to your career.

If you're a sprinter, someone who has exceptional bursts of energy and who can summon great concentration over short periods, you're good consultant material.

On the other hand, if you don't burn energy that intensely, and you work better in a steadier, more leisurely mode, you're possibly better employee material.

I'm a sprinter in most things, except sports. When I exercise, I like slow warm-ups, lengthy jogs, and high-repetition resistance workouts. I take my time.

Otherwise, I think fast, write quickly, and am generally a fast study. I have always been able to size up situations with very few clues. That's a good ability to have if you're a consultant.

****

I'm also suspicious of large bureaucracies, whether they're corporate or governmental. I don't trust them to take care of me.

A certain amount of paranoia was transmitted to me by my Dad. He was a highly educated career salesperson. He also ran radio stations and produced TV programs. And he was fiercely independent.

He performed exceedingly well, but he just didn't want the life that came with being a manager in a big organization. He taught me to be careful in dealing with them.

Although he didn't live to see the pain being inflicted upon workers by downsizing, reengineering, and massive layoffs, he would have seen these events as par for the course. He always felt the era of the Gold Watch would come to an end.

And it has. In a sense, these trends are making more and more people involuntary consultants. Numerous companies have terminated employees, only to turn around and hire them back as consultants. The second time around, however, the re-hired don't earn nearly as many dollars, perks, or health benefits.

Personnel firms report a booming business in what is called employee leasing. This is a hiring method that enables an employer to take on a person on a long-term but temporary basis. There is no assurance of ongoing employment beyond an agreed-upon period.

From the corporate perspective, it's cheaper and legally less risky to hire folks this way. Because workers don't have an expectation of permanent work, they're less likely to sue for wrongful termination when they're let go.

Some people believe that this is a megatrend of the future. They predict that companies will be staffed with hordes of virtual workers, whose contributions are permanent but whose physical presence is only fleeting.

If you buy in to this prophesy, one conclusion is apparent:

Sooner or later, most of us are going to become consultants.

So we may as well learn what it takes to perform well in this role.

****

Let's look at the lifestyle and activities of most consultants. They provide some important insights into this career, while demonstrating its pluses and minuses.

Consulting is often characterized as a feast-or-famine occupation. When you're on an assignment, you'll generally earn substantial money. But these periods of income can be separated by long or frequent periods of negative cash flows.

Your peak periods may enable you to squirrel away enough for the low times—if you're prudent. But being regularly unemployed might not be kind to your moods or to the peace of mind of your family and friends.

****

Let me give you a few examples from my experience. I consulted for a major firm over a period of two years. I was the third highest paid person in the company. Only the CEO and president earned more.

My fees had to be reported in the annual 10K report filed by public companies. We're not speaking of a great fortune, but we are speaking of very respectable executive pay.

And then, somewhat suddenly, it came to an end. The firm was bought by a cost-cutting conglomerate that didn't believe in consultants. Overtures were made to me about joining the firm as a formal employee, but I declined.

I hustled up some contracts after that, but it took eleven months of solid marketing to land my next big client. That contract lasted ten months, and was quite lucrative. Then, the doldrums settled in for about seven months, before my activity picked up again.

In seventeen years of consulting, the longest I've gone between major contracts has been about a year. What the heck did I do with myself during the lean times, you might wonder.

I went to law school, graduated, and passed the bar exam. Completed an advanced M.B.A. Traveled to Europe about six times. Wrote several books. Developed seminars and audio seminars. Published a newsletter.

And I worried, at least a little, about who my next client would be.

****

When times were good, I made offers on million-dollar-plus homes in tony spots like Pebble Beach. I drove a $150,000 Mercedes while casting condescending looks at the other two Mercedes that I owned.

When times weren't good, I had to lay off helpers, reduce telephone lines into my office, cancel subscriptions and professional memberships, shrink donations to my favorite colleges, and watch the proverbial pennies.

Get the picture?

It reminds me of the famous line from Dickens:

Consulting ushers in the best of times, and the worst of times.

When you're a consultant, you'll be utterly amazed at how quickly you traverse these polarities.

****

Of course, this is the same teeter-totter that actors, writers, artists, commission salespeople, and the self-employed ride. Good times and bad times.

A scene from my recent experience tells the story.

"Welcome home, Dr. Goodman," the gracious concierge said.

It had been a tough day at the office—not mine, but a client's. It reminded me of the old aspirin commercials.

Tension, pressure, pain.

It didn't help that my rented Chrysler convertible had been transformed into a life raft. While I was working with my client over the course of nine hours, one of the Gulf Coast's hurricanes had inundated the streets with ten inches of rain.

Intersections looked like jagged boat docks. Beached cars were everywhere, like paralyzed whales. I was lucky I reached my destination.

And now, as the concierge had gently reminded me, I was home, if not entirely dry. I suppose if you do a little math, you could call it home.

I spent four to five days of every week, for about a year and a half, in Houston on a major consulting contract. When we first got underway, I would wearily check in and out of various hotels.

But then, I discovered the Four Seasons.

It was one of the nicest hotels in town, although it was about twenty minutes from my client's site when we had reasonable weather. The Four Seasons had allocated about one-half of its suites for use as apartments for businesspeople such as me.

It was no more expensive to rent these lavish units by the month than to check in and out of lesser hotels. It saved time, provided all the services I needed, plus it was attached by tunnels to a mall and to a health club.

I didn't suffer.

✳✳✳✳✳✳✳✳✳✳

All in all, most experienced consultants live an upscale life when they're on the road. I usually fly business or first class. It is a far cry from my early days as a consultant, when I would drive from town to town for weeks at a time. Back then, staying at a Motel 6 was the best I could afford.

Travel seems to be part of the package if you choose to consult. As Peter Drucker pointed out to me, "As a consultant, your business always seems to be where you aren't!"

The consulting lifestyle can certainly range from the ridiculous to the sublime. And I think I've experienced it all in my years in this wonderful, challenging, and unpredictable field.

I think consulting can make a superb second career, providing it fits your temperament, skills, ambitions, and lifestyle. This book will help you to determine if consulting is for you, while showing you how consultants work, live, and think.

I'll also show you how to break into the field.

It isn't the civil service—that I can tell you. But like a tempestuous but exhilarating interpersonal relationship, the good times usually make up for the bad.

That's if you do your job right. And that's what this book is about—showing you the way.

Experiences and Skills That Prepare You for Consulting

How are consultants made?

There are several good breeding grounds for consultants:

M.B.A. Programs

There are people who fly through college, earn a B.A. or a B.S., and then immediately sign on for an M.B.A. program. If they are highly ranked in their classes they can qualify for junior roles in major consulting firms, such as McKinsey, Ernst and Young, Andersen, and Coopers and Lybrand.

It takes time for these recent graduates to move up in the firm, and their pay is reasonably good: $60,000+ to start. But they have to be willing to fly or drive everywhere and live out of a suitcase.

Academia

Many business school professors moonlight as consultants. They see consulting as providing a nice income supplement to their guaranteed professorial salaries.

However, professors are severely limited in the time they can invest with clients because of their university duties. In some locales, state university professors can't allocate more than a small proportion of their time to outside consulting projects.

Nonetheless, being a professor, or having been one, is a leg up on consulting. Here are some of the strengths academics bring to this second career:

* They're analytical, by training.

* Some possess excellent training skills.

* They're often skilled at handling school politics, which one of my professors claimed was a more taxing undertaking than governmental politics.

* They're positively predisposed to the life cycle associated with consulting work. Its beginning-middle-end format is consistent with the closed-ended calendar found in teaching.

* They're used to being accorded high intellectual status and power, by virtue of their academic positions.

* They have often earned advanced degrees, which accord them a certain degree of credibility and clout.

* They only have students for short periods of time, so they're used to trying to effectuate major improvements in achievement, quickly.

* Academic salaries are relatively low. Consulting wages are relatively high, even when taking into account the feast/famine cycles I've described for you. So, consulting is often a step up.

There are some drawbacks to consulting. With some clients, the more academic credentials you have, the less esteem they give you. You can be seen as an egghead, or as a thinker and not a doer.

You know the old saw about those who can, do; while those

who can't, teach. Especially in situations where one is dealing with people without college backgrounds, having academic standing or experience can be seen as a minus.

For instance, before I was starting a nationwide training program for an airline, I was warned by my contact, a marketing manager, to drop the Dr. title in front of my name.

He didn't mean that I should invite people to call me Gary, which I like, anyway. He didn't want them to know I had a Ph.D.! I agreed, of course, but I did ask him about his reasoning.

He said, "Things will go better for you, that's all."

Some professors are like drill sergeants when they're in a classroom, and they expect to be able to command-and-control civilians in corporate life. It just doesn't work like that.

How much you are liked is often more important in determining your attractiveness as a consultant than how right your ideas are.

Donald Petersen, the former CEO of Ford Motor Company, said it well when he pointed out that the number-one reason people get ahead in companies is due to their skill at getting along with others. He has also seen more promising careers flameout because of poor people skills than for any other reason.

So if you want to consult for the primary purpose of appearing to be a know-it-all, this motivation will backfire. People generally react defensively to outsiders, anyway. If you come in with a chip on your shoulder, you'll only worsen their moods and stiffen their opposition to change.

Notwithstanding these potential problems, teaching can be a good training ground for future consultants.

Any Field in Which You Have Extensive Experience or Expertise

I was fortunate to have received early training in telephone sales and management from Time/Life.

By age 19, I had already become our region's number-one salesperson, and when a management slot opened up, I moved up. Before long, I was responsible for nearly everything the office did, twelve hours per day, five days a week, plus a half day on Saturday.

I recruited, trained, supervised, coached, counseled, compensated, and otherwise held the hands of sixty people, including the back office staff.

It was intense but invaluable experience. I recall suggesting to my boss that we try consulting in the area of telemarketing to other firms.

His response was, "Nah, they wouldn't see the benefit." And his opinion was accurate until America was pummeled by two oil embargoes. Then, businesses became very interested in learning how to do more things by phone, to save gas and money.

By the time that had happened, I had earned three degrees, including the Ph.D. in communications from the University of Southern California. So, I combined meaningful experience and true expertise with academic insights and advanced degrees.

The result was big-time credibility.

✸✸✸✸✸✸✸✸✸✸

I was lucky, inasmuch as I saw my calling very early in life. I sensed that I wanted to consult, so I formulated an action plan for preparing myself to skillfully pursue it. Nonetheless, to enter the field properly, it had to be a second career, for me.

While I was pursuing my Ph.D., I racked up years of classroom teaching experience. So by the time I launched my consulting practice, I had a veritable cache of lecture units that I could blend with my telemarketing know-how.

I merged these assets into what I called a Telephone Effectiveness Workshop, a one-day program that I convinced thirty-five universities across the country to sponsor.

That gave me publicity and stature and led to consulting contracts with big companies such as Xerox, Polaroid, and General Foods, to name a few.

A major book publisher discovered my classes and invited me to write a book based upon my expertise. I did a lot better than that!

Six of my titles were published over a five-year period.

Some went on to achieve best-seller status, and this helped me to secure even more clients.

And a cycle of consulting at a fairly high level resulted.

✳✳✳✳✳✳✳✳✳✳

If you're accomplished in any field, you can take your knowledge and, literally, sell it back to the industry that endowed you with it in the first place.

Recently, Time/Life sent four managers to attend one of my public seminars in Orlando. A few months later, *Time* magazine anointed me a small business expert and began publishing my articles on its Internet site.

So, you *can* go home again!

✳✳✳✳✳✳✳✳✳✳

In America, we have one of the most advanced systems of formal education in the world. Our universities are attended by legions of foreign students who recognize a bargain when they see one.

But our vocational education system leaves a lot to be desired. Apprenticeship programs are rare, but they're plentiful in Europe and in other countries. This means there are tons of opportunities for people to enter the field of consulting if they can package a cost-effective vocational training program.

That's what I did with telephone training. People aren't born telephonically effective. They have to learn, yet there are exceedingly few classes found in this area in formal education channels.

This left a vacuum that I could fill, and I exploited it.

✳✳✳✳✳✳✳✳✳✳

Let me describe another vacuum that one of my clients has begun to occupy. He looked around and noticed that there was a steady supply of one type of person—the unemployed or the job-changer.

And the more senior the person, the longer it takes for him

or her to find placement. This is complicated by the fact that this sort of high-powered individual isn't unemployed often enough to sharpen his job-hunting skills, and you have a perfect opportunity for a consultant.

The consultant I know decided to carve out a very narrow area of expertise:

He writes resumes for job-seekers.

And he stays very, very busy. His service costs under $200, but it is worth tens, if not hundreds of thousands to the job-seeker who lands a position with a polished resume.

Years ago, at a consulting convention where I was a featured speaker, I ran into a fellow who decided to consult in the area of how to start home-based businesses. Frankly, at the time, I was oblivious to the opportunity that he saw with 20/20 clarity.

I was busy courting big companies. He wasn't. He noticed a demographic trend that pointed to the creation of millions of new jobs in microbusinesses. Every meaningful statistic he uncovered pointed to a boom that was starting to get underway in businesses that operate out of garages, spare bedrooms, and the corners of living rooms.

It was slow-going, at first. But he and his wife hung on, and within a few years they published a best-selling book on the topic. They also developed a flourishing consulting practice advising people on how they could work effectively from their homes.

Peter Drucker, one of my professors and an acknowledged management guru, has said that no one can see the future. All we can hope to do, as entrepreneurs, is to see what has already happened, that no one else has really noticed.

Viewed this way, nearly anything can be a field for the prospective consultant.

The Economics of Consulting

The other day, I was called by a major computer company that wants an advanced telemarketing seminar for twenty of its people.

The program will occur during a two- to three-hour period. I can fly in and out the same day. Of course, I was asked what my fee would be.

Forty-five hundred dollars, plus travel expenses.

Do you think that's a lot of money for a two- to three-hour hour speech?

I don't. And most professional consultants would agree with me.

Here are the economic considerations involved in this assignment.

It takes substantially more time than three hours to deliver the program they want.

The site is in Dallas, and I'm starting from L.A. So right off the bat, we have a two-hour time difference. I have to catch a 7 A.M. flight to arrive at approximately 11:30–noon.

Assuming I'm met by a car at the airport, I'll have just enough time to make it to the site and to begin the program at 1 P.M. If I hope to catch a 5 or 5:30 flight back, the latest I can end is at 4 P.M. I'll arrive at about 6:30, and then face a one-hour trip back to my home.

So when you factor in travel to and from airports, I will have been on the job from at least 5 A.M. until 7 P.M. my time. That's a tight and tense fourteen-hour day.

It's really two days, compressed into one. So, my fee is transformed from $4,500 for a three-hour talk, into $4,500 for two days. But let's not stop there.

I haven't factored in a minute for preparing the speech and coordinating the subject matter and travel details with the company's contact, right?

Given my passion for being prepared, you can allocate another day for building the speech, studying the audience, and customizing the units to meet their needs.

So, the $4,500 is divided into three days, which means a fee of roughly $1,500 per day.

But there are other factors that need to be considered before we end our analysis of that number: expertise and overhead.

I have over twenty years of experience in telemarketing. Five college degrees, and some very special know-how about dealing with this client's very demanding professional audience of 20 souls.

Should there be some extra acknowledgment of these unique abilities in the form of above-average compensation?

But let me share a classic story with you that is a more eloquent defense of the consultant's fee structure.

✳✳✳✳✳✳✳✳✳✳

A large ship was stuck in dry dock because its engines weren't working. The chief engineer couldn't solve the problem, so he reluctantly brought in a consultant.

The hired gun looked high and low, and then finally pointed to one spot. "That's where your problem is," he said.

He pulled a small hammer from his pocket. Then he began a simple but steady tapping action near the turbine.

Suddenly, the engine roared to life, and within minutes the ship was making its way out of the harbor. When the chief engineer received the consultant's bill, it read as follows:

Tapping:	$ 1.00
Knowing where to tap:	9,999.00
BALANCE DUE:	$10,000.00
Thank You!	

One of the problems with selling knowledge or expertise is that it's an intangible to the buyer. All the chief engineer saw was a short period of tapping with a cheap hammer.

The temptation is to declare, Why, any child knows how to tap!

But the consultant's retort is, "Surely, but he doesn't know where to tap."

✳✳✳✳✳✳✳✳✳✳

The consultant in this illustration has difficulty dramatizing the value of his work. Yet this is a very significant requirement if he is to get paid and to earn enough to survive.

It's ironic that many corporations exhort their employees to work smart, but they often resent it when an outsider, in the form of a consultant, does it, and then charges accordingly.

If you're not visibly sweating, or putting in long hours in front of clients, it is easy for them to underestimate your contribution. So to have a future in consulting, you need to develop skill in explaining how you arrived at your fees.

✱✱✱✱✱✱✱✱✱✱

Expertise and experience should be rewarded. But there is a second justification for one's fees: overhead.

Every business has it. It is a simple word that captures all of the costs associated with delivering your product to your client. I'm not going to itemize all of the overhead costs of consulting, but suffice it to say that the average consultant's overhead has been estimated at eighty dollars per hour.

In other words, for each eight-hour consulting day that is on the clock, the consultant forks out the equivalent of $640. This means that she doesn't start earning a living until she charges more than this figure.

But this subject grows more complicated than doing simple arithmetic. Here's why: Consultants don't usually bill for all of their time.

They have marketing time. It could easily take an hour of marketing to obtain an hour of consulting work; sometimes, a lot more. So consultants aren't seeing income during much of their time.

Yet they need to hold themselves in readiness to perform, should a client call upon them. They have to be available to work.

Let's be optimistic and assume that a full-time consultant will be able to bill twenty-five hours per week. Say he wishes to earn $75,000, after expenses. How much will he have to charge per hour or per day?

There are 1,200 billable hours during his fifty-week year, allowing two weeks for vacation. To net $75,000, he has to charge sixty dollars on top of his eighty dollars overhead for a total per hour of $140. This means he needs to bill at a minimum of $1,120 per day.

If he wants $150,000 per year, he needs to bill at $200 per hour, or $1,600 per day. And I must emphasize, he needs to be billing slightly more than three full days of consulting per week.

This is achievable. I have been able to bill nearly every day of the month when working on intensive jobs for clients. This is one way to get ahead so you can afford the slow times.

And there are variants of the hourly billing arrangement.

I decided, early in my career, not to sell my time by the hour. Instead, I chose to make it available in daily units.

Looking back at my example of the Dallas speech, what would the result be if the client asked, "What do you charge per hour?" Prorating my fee, I could have said, "$200" or "$250."

"Okay," he says, sensing a bargain, "we want three hours of your time in Dallas."

How could I even do that speech, the preparation required, and the travel, for $600-$750? Impossible. As it was, quoting $4,500 plus travel for a speech didn't sound nearly as reasonable as it is.

Because I'm flying in and out the same day, it still appears to require only a single day of my time. And that's an illusion.

✳✳✳✳✳✳✳✳✳✳

There are consultants who bill by the project, especially if it is going to take place over a long time span, say several weeks or months.

It's like being a house painter and quoting a flat fee for the job. Seldom will painters say, "I charge $ __ per hour." They bid the job, and their obligation is to bring it in for that price, no matter how long it takes.

I know a consultant who only charges $1,000 to $1,200 per day. You might wonder how he can get by with such a small return.

He told me that he plays a shell game. While the client is watching one hand, which is extending a low daily rate, the other hand is designing a program that requires oodles of days.

For instance, it might take me five days to do a job. He'll

take the same opportunity and bill fifteen days for it. Frankly, I think his methods aren't nearly as sophisticated as mine, and so it does take him more time to show results.

But he's also packing it in. He has actually had his prospects phone me to ask about my daily rate so he could exclaim, "See, I'm a lot cheaper than he is!"

Unsophisticated clients don't believe You Get What You Pay For. They believe that human services are fungible, which means that vendors are roughly equivalent in abilities and effectiveness. Therefore, they comparison-shop fees. This exerts a practical limitation upon what you can charge.

Scott Turow, the lawyer turned best-selling novelist, expressed the view of most clients when he disclosed his belief, when speaking of lawyers. He asserted, "No human being is worth $300 per hour!"

I think he's completely wrong. Value is an extremely slippery concept. We've all heard the expression, A word to the wise is sufficient. It should also be worth a lot, if it is the right word uttered by a professional consultant.

One of my clients hired me to improve his telemarketing unit that was promoting personalized gift wrapping to retailers. These are rolls of wrapping paper with people's names on them. So, if someone is giving presents to Mary, the giver can purchase gift wrapping with Mary's name on it. Nice idea.

Well, this fellow came to me with another product that he wanted to sell by phone. It is a water purifier that looks like a ballpoint pen. By pressing a button at the tip of the cylinder, the user can administer a drop of a chemical compound that treats the water so it becomes safe to drink.

He said to me, excitedly, "I think we can retail it for $69.95, and I can get them very cheaply overseas. Can we sell it by phone?"

I thought about it for a minute, and I said, "Yes, you can sell it by phone, but it's not economically viable." In other words, I nixed the idea.

I had my reasons. First, it was a true innovation. Innovations are very, very difficult to pioneer exclusively by phone. Prospects would need to see the item, so ads would have to be taken out, or brochures created.

Because it was new, people would be distrustful of a gizmo that claimed certain health-giving benefits. Endorsements would need to be obtained from credible experts before prospects would invest their trust.

Moreover, this item represented a departure from the way people purchase pure water now in bottles or through filters. Sellers would have to argue against these entrenched methods to establish the superiority of theirs.

(I did perceive a potential niche market: travelers to other countries. They're always concerned about pure water, so advertising the device in airline and travel publications might be the best way to go, initially.)

I shared these thoughts with the client. He was in a state of near shock that I could dismiss his idea so rapidly, and conclusively.

I did him a big favor. He would have invested tens of thousands of dollars in an utter loser, if I hadn't set him straight. So, let's get back to the compensation question:

How much was my one minute of reflection and judgment worth?

The answer is, infinitely more than I can charge for it.

✳✳✳✳✳✳✳✳✳✳

As a young man, Henry Ford labored in one of Thomas Edison's factories. Ford had a burning question that he wanted desperately to ask Mr. Edison. The answer could change history.

One day, Edison was brusquely moving through the factory when young Ford jumped in his way and asked:

Mr. Edison: Do you think the gasoline engine is a suitable power plant for an automobile?

Reportedly, Edison snapped back: YES!

That is the proverbial word to the wise, in action. How many billions of dollars do you think that answer was worth?

It only helped to launch the modern auto industry!

✳✳✳✳✳✳✳✳✳✳

So, what is the value that clients are purchasing from consultants? It goes well beyond time, as we can see.

They're buying know-how, availability, and judgment.

If you bring these strengths to clients, you'll be a good consultant. If you get your clients to understand that this is what they're truly buying, you'll become a prosperous one, as well.

In the next chapter, we'll explore the psychology of consulting. You'll learn what it takes to prepare for the inner game of this sensational second career.

2

The Psychology of Consulting

*T*his chapter should be titled, "Always a Bridesmaid, Never a Bride." Because one of the iron facts of consulting is that you are usually in the wings, whispering tips into the ears of your clients. You don't get much time, if any, at center stage, yourself.

And if you do find yourself in the limelight, it is fleeting, or it is for the purpose of being a scapegoat.

Perhaps an even more appropriate moniker for this section could be "How Clients Use Consultants," because this sheds light upon the psychology of the relationship a consultant has to his patrons and to his work.

****

Why do people hire consultants?

There are official as well as unofficial reasons.

Officially, consultants bring these attributes to an assignment:

Objectivity

They're outsiders, so they aren't part of the problem. If anyone can see, without bias, what's going on in an organization, it is the stranger.

The other day, I was speaking to someone who was having trouble with his boss. The boss had officially retired, but had been reincarnated as a consultant. His purported task was to oversee operations until a permanent replacement could be found.

Acting as a consultant, the boss was mucking things up by failing to support his former division. Suddenly, he was behaving like a statesman, whose responsibility was to the organization at large, and not to his unit.

I listened to this problem and inferred that the ex-incumbent-turned-consultant had a very different set of priorities than what my contact thought. He wasn't going to simply fade away when a replacement manager was appointed. He'd continue to try to get consulting work from the firm.

So, instead of seeing him as a passing problem, I counseled my contact to assume that he was going to hang around in one form or another.

TRANSLATION: Don't piss him off, because he'll have the clout to make your life hell.

My contact had never considered this scenario. I explained my vision by reminding him that I'm an outsider, so I don't operate from the same set of assumptions he does as a part of the system.

Special Skills

The most sound rationale for bringing in a consultant is the fact that she knows things that you don't. If you took the time to learn what she already knows, it would be costly and extremely inefficient. So you trade money for know-how and expediency.

I'm looking into doing some minor remodeling of the exterior of my home. Nothing serious, but it will expand the amount of usable yard that I currently have.

The city in which I live has a building permit process that can give any reasonable person fits. On another occasion, I went to get a permit on my own, and I heard four different sets of requirements in an hour and a half, from four different functionaries.

I believe I have found an architect/designer to help me out. She has done a number of tasteful jobs in my neighborhood. She knows the people at the building department. Given her connections and her ability to shepherd the process through, she'll be worth every penny of her consulting fee.

If you can do what others can't, this will be one of the strongest official justifications for bringing you aboard.

Of course there are some hefty motivations for bringing you in that are only tangentially related to the official reasons.

Here are the unofficial reasons you'll get a consulting project:

1. **You can be kept on a short leash.** If you're hired on a daily basis, your job terminates, and must be renewed daily. This gives you a greater incentive to please your master than a permanent employee might have.

Or, if you're hired to do a project and things sour, you can be paid off and you'll have to ride off into the sunset. So the sense of control is high for the person who hires a consultant.

2. **You won't be around to hog the credit if your involvement is a hit.** Your sponsor will claim it. After all, it was his idea to do the project, and he made the right personnel choice in executing it.

No one will name a hallway or a cafeteria after you, or send your name to the media as the heroic architect of sweeping change. To borrow from General MacArthur, you'll be a not-so-old soldier who will just fade away.

3. **You can bear the blame if the project fails.** Insiders will want to distance themselves from a losing venture, so they'll blame the consultant if things don't turn out right. Of course, these very insiders may have sabotaged the project, but you'll still be the object of their vitriol.

4. **You can be brought in to do the dirty jobs.** Imagine working as a manager for a firm for many years. Over that time, you've come to know your associates pretty well. You have attended company functions, like picnics, together.

Gone through thick and thin, together. But suddenly, the shareholders are clamoring for a higher stock price. The only way you can manufacture instant profits is by cost-cutting.

And the fastest way to do that is by slashing head-count. Suddenly, you have to tell your quasi-pals that they're going to be vaporized in the interest of the greater good.

Can't bring yourself around to doing it? Hire a consultant to recommend it, and then simply follow his board-approved action plan.

This same process is used time and again to introduce change that managers don't believe they can accomplish on their own. Consultants are the tool to accomplishing difficult and sometimes necessary outcomes that the company simply can't promote from within.

5. **You might even be brought in to fail.** Let's say a senior manager gets the brilliant idea that telemarketers should be brought in to replace field salespeople. The sales manager is asked to bring in a consultant. He doesn't want to, but he realizes his career will be toast if he balks.

So, he hires a consultant to do a pilot program. The pilot is booby-trapped. The worst prospects are selected for telemarketing attention. Deliveries are late, resulting in customer complaints. It appears that customers just won't accept this new way of doing business.

The sales manager can report to his boss that, "We tried, but I guess it just didn't work!"

****

While some of these dynamics could appear to be negatives, they are counterbalanced by positives.

First, you are a short-timer at any given client's locale. This means you should have the role-distance to make the difficult decisions without worrying about reprisals as co-employees would.

Without the concern of job security, you might actually try harder and achieve more than the typical employee. Because your contributions are being assessed every twenty-four hours, you're probably putting more into and getting more out of each day.

In other words, you're living in dog years, i.e., every year of work for you is equivalent to seven by an employee.

Of course, as a consultant you're also being given more problems to solve than a typical employee. This variety of circumstances, and the accompanying sense of novelty they create, can keep you very interested in your work.

Yet there is a special psychology in being a temp, whether you're operating as a highly paid, short-term expert, or even a word processor. You need to be highly fluid, and fit into different situations immediately.

You also need to be able to slip out of them, and return to your perennial job hunt with peace of mind, or adapt to the next assignment, all in the blink of an eye.

And you can't afford to grow attached to a given client. When I invest many months with a company, it is almost impossible not to identify with its values and build relationships with co-workers.

This is normal and human. Probably healthy, too. But it's dangerous, psychologically, if you overidentify with your sponsors, because you'll run the risk of trying to elongate a contract when you should leave.

You can't ever get so sentimental as to make leaving a big deal, emotionally. I probably go to extremes to avoid this problem.

At one site, where I had spent over a year, by the time my last day came, I didn't announce it to anyone or bring any extra attention to it. My key contacts were aware of the fact that the contract had concluded.

To avoid making a scene, I had gradually deconstructed my office over the previous few weeks, so all I had to carry away was my computer, in its handy carrying case, over my shoulder. I walked to the elevator, pushed the button, and vanished.

No balloons, no cake, no parties, no streamers, and no tears.

Parting can be sorrowful, but it can also be welcomed. Once you have made your contribution, to hang around may seem to put a few extra bucks into your pocket, but it isn't appreciated by your sponsors if they believe you're just trying to line your pockets.

Of course, comings and goings are important rituals, and there might be occasions during which farewells might be more formal or warmer. But I haven't had all that many, as a consultant.

****

Let me analogize this situation to a preventive dental procedure that I was advised to have. I was referred to a periodontist, who was cheerful, actually humorous, and who seemed like a real pro.

The operation was performed with a local anesthetic, but it wasn't comfortable. The post-op care that I had to perform on my own was also a pain.

During one follow-up visit, the periodontist seemed to be fishing for a compliment with regard to the success of the operation. I didn't feel like gushing about the experience. He was good; don't get me wrong.

But I didn't sing his praises to my friends and neighbors because the dental experience, while effective, wasn't something I wanted to relive, if only in my mind.

I believe lots of people feel this way about consultants, teachers, accountants, and numerous professional people from whom they seek help.

People use their services because they must. But the second they can fire them, they do so. Perhaps a part of the psychology that operates in this context is the fact that we resent having to obtain outside assistance.

Possibly it deflates our egos, or it makes us feel vulnerable. If we could, we'd fix our own teeth, take our own advice, and do our own taxes. The desire to feel independent is deeply embedded in most people.

Frankly, we just don't feel very safe or confident about depending upon outsiders for the satisfaction of our needs. So it's easy to feel that clients are always trying to fire me, when I serve them as a consultant.

Because they are.

✱✱✱✱✱✱✱✱✱✱

If gratitude is what you're looking for, consulting won't provide much of it. I recall hearing an attorney say that he believed that he needed to get his clients to pay their statements promptly because the half-life of their gratitude can be measured in hours.

In other words, they forget about your contribution very rapidly. In consulting, you'll find that after you're gone, clients will come to believe that they developed most of your good ideas and procedures themselves!

They'll take the credit, and they might even deny that you did them any good. This is a problem, because if your clients can't see the value you added, how are they going to recommend you to your next employer?

Most of us who work for other people depend upon our references. If we can't get past employers to say nice things about us, we'll find getting more work very difficult. This is an added detriment to consulting.

Not only are your past clients unlikely to become permanently impressed with your efforts on their behalf, but they are also reluctant to share you with other companies, especially in their own industries.

I heard one consultant say, "It's easy to get the first assignment in an industry, but it's nearly impossible to get the second."

This means that it's difficult to do what lots of businesses attempt to do: to exploit customer niches. If you can't get the second client from the same sector, how can you exploit what you've learned from the first?

You can't, at least directly. Through a technology-transfer kind of process you can borrow from one industry and graft the innovation upon another.

This is healthy for the economy at large, because it disseminates learning much as a bee pollinates flowers. If you're an employee instead of a consultant, you're almost expected to stay in the same basic industry, as long as you don't sign a noncompete or trade secrets agreement to the contrary.

Look at it from the point of your sponsors. You have learned a lot about them and their methods. Do they want to help you to blab to their competitors?

You might think that they'd have no problem crowing about your achievements to noncompetitors, right? It doesn't work this way, for a few reasons.

One is jealousy. If you were so good, they must have been really needy, and less capable. This insight threatens their self-images. Secondly, many consulting clients will utilize your help and then fantasize about becoming consultants themselves.

I can't tell you how many of my sponsors in client companies actually tried to do my act on their own, as consultants, after our contracts had concluded. You'd be amazed at the number.

So don't expect rave reviews for your work. The fact that you worked for Meglo Motors Corporation may be a credential that's worth less than you hoped.

Your key contact may be prevented by the corporation from touting your work to other firms that might inquire about you. They could be paranoid that their trade secrets will be revealed, or that you might actually sue them for providing negative information about your work.

But this is a fact that you need to be aware of. You may not have as many boosters as you feel you should, given the quality of your exertions.

Sort Out Your Values and You'll Succeed

If I'm painting a portrait of a field that is emotionally taxing, then I'm getting my point across. An even better way of dramatizing the point may be to help you to understand your values before you choose consulting as a second career.

When I was a college professor I helped my students to analyze their motivations as well as those of audiences by using a listing of key values.

Instead of going through all of them, I'd like to point out a few that are implicated in the life of a consultant.

****

One of your most important values could be a sense of belonging. It is in the top quartile of values for many people. They like to feel part of a team. They enjoy camaraderie and sharing, and they feel that they have a common destiny with others in their community and work group.

They love the good cheer of buying balloons and ice cream for fellow employees' birthday parties. The worst part of being out sick, or on vacation, is the fact that they miss the office gossip and social interaction.

If this seems to describe you, you may not want to become a consultant. Because you're constantly coming and going, hiring onto and then being terminated from organizations, this cycle could certainly militate against bonding with others.

****

On the other hand, if you hold dear another value, independence, then consulting might be a peachy occupation. That's one of the key payoffs of being an advisor-for-hire. You're a rolling stone.

Independence, and the sense of freedom it brings, are very, very important to me.

****

Now let's make this a little more complicated. People don't have just one value. We have lots of them, and the key to knowing ourselves and living a rewarding life is to rank them in the order of their importance to us.

Then, when there's a conflict between values, we'll know which one to choose. For instance, a prosperous life may be something that you and I would both like to achieve.

But what if our desire for independence prevents us from earning the consistently high salaries that we could command if we were 9-to-5ers? Would you sacrifice your need to feel independent for the guaranteed money offered by a regular job?

I'm not sure I would. I think I'd rather scale down my spending to conform to my income, while retaining a feeling of freedom. Or, simply sell more deals to more companies, for that matter.

****

There is another value worth discussing: social recognition. This is the high opinion of others.

Consulting can cut both ways with respect to this value. On the one hand, being a consultant seems to say to the world that you're smart. After all, companies respect your opinion enough to seek your advice and to pay big bucks for the privilege.

To the person next door, this may seem like a very upscale career. And it can be.

But, as I pointed out earlier in this chapter, you may not earn the long-lasting recognition or respect from your clients that you'd like.

****

Family security is another value that calls for discussion. Is consulting family-friendly? If you have to spend most of your professional life on airplanes and in hotels, I'm not so sure.

Absence may make the heart grow fonder, but it can put a heck of a strain upon relationships. As a Dad, I can tell you that being completely present might be the best present I can give to those I love.

****

There is another side to the coin. It's possible to earn veritable windfalls of money in consulting. You could develop a niche that is extremely lucrative.

There have been stages in my consulting career when I've

been able to get ahead of the game, financially. This capability to bring in significant sums over short periods enabled me to afford down payments on houses and my office property.

Had I been stuck in a typical job, no matter how well-paying, I wouldn't have had the flexibility to wheel-and-deal as I have.

I suppose I'm not describing anything that any small businessperson doesn't know. When you work for yourself, you not only incur downside risks, but upside potential, as well.

So, family security can be enhanced by virtue of a consultant's ability to generate large infusions of cash. Moreover, with some limitations, a consultant can enhance his or her family's security by choosing to live and work in a location that has family benefits.

As a consultant, you can choose to live or work anywhere. Want to live at the beach, or snugly sequester yourself into the mountains? You can do it.

You can work from home, or from a high-rise.

✷✷✷✷✷✷✷✷✷✷

When I was finishing my Ph.D., I toured the very impressive Century City high-rise offices of some fellow Ph.D.s who had just launched a consulting practice.

They beamed as they showed me the big desks they had rented, and their large, red swivel chairs. Even their workroom, with its fancy postage meter, looked impressive!

The rent on the place was $2,000 per month, which, eighteen years ago, was BIG MONEY. Of course, they asserted that all of the fancy window dressing was necessary. BIG CLIENTS would be attracted to it, and they'd find its occupants credible.

I left, impressed, but also queasy. I wouldn't have wanted the overhead that they were burdening themselves with. And I promised myself that if I were going to invest that kind of money in a property, I'd own it.

That didn't happen overnight. My first office was no more than a spare bedroom in our apartment, but it worked for me. I was deeply into jogging at the time, and the apartment was located only a few blocks from Glendale College's beautiful track.

So I'd awaken at 5, make some long-distance calls until 7, and then put in about five to six miles on the track each morning. I'd return to eat breakfast, and then to put in another eight or nine hours of work.

It was great. I watched every penny, but my overhead was minuscule.

What happened to my Century City colleagues? Within four years, they folded their operation, which was heavily in debt. I bought myself an office building with the money I had saved on rent!

My office is about three miles from my house. On occasion, I've walked to it when my car has been in the shop. I can reach a million businesses within an hour's drive.

I'm fifteen minutes from the Burbank Airport. Glendale, where I'm located, is reputed to be one of the safest cities of its size in America.

But if I felt it would be better for my family to move operations tomorrow, I could. That's the beauty of being a consultant.

Becoming a Consultant Isn't a One-Way Street

Lots of consultants choose this profession reluctantly.

Many have come from an aerospace or engineering background. They're educated, and they have very specialized knowledge.

But how many bombers and space shuttles and Hubble Telescopes can we build? When funding dries up because of the cessation of a Cold War, or because of recessions or political budget battles, many of these specialists become unemployed.

Their only viable choice is to package their know-how and to sell it, or even rent it, to employers. Thus consultants are born.

I had been a college professor for four years when I decided to hang out my consulting shingle. I made a calculated decision that I wanted to schedule courses by the day instead of by the semester.

I also wanted to upgrade my financial situation. Consulting

enabled me to feel truly free for the first time. I was free to earn, grow, create, market, and simply THINK.

If I wanted to spend hours, days, weeks, or months reading in libraries, I could.

At the same time that I was attracted to these aspects of consulting, I realized the time had come when I had to change careers. College teaching had lost its magic. I just couldn't get along anymore communicating mostly to audiences of eighteen- to twenty-one-year-olds.

Pleasantly, there was no exam to pass before I could call myself a consultant. I didn't need anyone's approval or blessing.

No insurmountable economic hurdles existed. The fundamental thing that makes you a consultant is the same asset that makes any business: clients.

And there are many people who take advantage of this fact when they select consulting as an occupation. They can enter it, or leave it, for that matter, very easily.

****

Many consultants use their mobility and freedom to scope out firms with which they would consider permanent employment. If they're hired on for a project, and they do well, they might lobby for a permanent position.

That hasn't been my objective, but it works for lots of people. They see consulting as transitional, and it can be an excellent way of gaining compensation while one seeks new, and even more stable, opportunities.

I ran into a consultant who helped to turn around a software company that had gotten into financial difficulties. He assisted in trimming the payroll by a third. By the time the firm was on a better footing, he was named president of one of its divisions.

Was this his aim all along? Could be.

There are companies that hire people on a consulting basis for the primary purpose of road-testing them for potential permanent employment, later. If they don't come up to snuff, there is no stigma associated with letting them go, because it appeared that their tenure was limited, by design.

And there are people who move back and forth from formal

employment to consulting status across their entire working lives. If it works for them, that's great.

I recall speaking to a relative a few months ago when we got onto the subject of employment versus consulting. He mentioned that he was great at interviewing for jobs. He boasted that over 90 percent of his interviews, as a young man, resulted in job offers.

He mentioned that he would like the consulting lifestyle, but he feared that many companies were anticonsulting. So, he might not work for the firms he really respected if he hung out his shingle.

I suggested he think of himself as a consultant, but interview as a prospective employee. For the firms that wanted people to be on board with both feet, he could convey that sense of permanence.

Yet, mentally, he might plan on staying with any particular firm for no more than two to three years. This way, he could have psychological role-distance, and not feel that his choice of work at a given time was forever and ever.

Knowing it was closed-ended could enable him to feel comfortable, come what may. If it was terrific, great. He could mentally renew his psychological employment contract with the firm, without saying a word to anyone.

If not, his bags would never be completely unpacked.

It's up to us to determine what we need, emotionally and intellectually, from our work. Do we need permanence and beautiful high-rises in which to feel secure?

Or, do we need to feel that we're, fundamentally, on our own?

You can have either or both through consulting. It's your choice, and that's nice to know.

In the next chapter, we'll talk about the crucial business of marketing your consulting practice.

3

Marketing Your Consulting Services

I had the privilege of seeing the fine actor Jeremy Brett bring his role of Sherlock Holmes to live audiences on stage in London's West End. He dazzled us then just as he had dazzled us through numerous television episodes.

In the play, Holmes was tormented by depression and melancholy, and the brightest note in the entire production was heard right after the doorbell rang. Holmes rejoiced, Aha, a Client!

I grinned, because that's exactly how excited I feel when I've landed a good account. It's completely joyful, because I get to ply my trade. I come alive when I'm undertaking an ambitious consulting relationship.

And so will you. But of course, the big question is: How can you get that doorbell to ring, or how should you go out and ring the bells so you generate clients on a regular basis? That's what we'll address in this chapter.

Marketing Makes the Difference

When I was working on a major consulting contract for the U.S. Navy, one of my colleagues exclaimed, over dinner and drinks:

The only meaningful difference between consultants is marketing!

I don't know if I'd agree 100 percent, but I would say that marketing is the crucial variable that determines whether a consultant will succeed or fail.

In the last chapter, I mentioned that few clients will spontaneously sing your praises to others, so word-of-mouth advertising is nearly nonexistent. Just because your mind works like a steel trap doesn't mean you'll snare any business without effort and cunning.

You could be brilliant and penniless!

But you'll thrive if you make it easy for customers to discover you.

Arno Penzias, Nobel laureate and chief scientist for AT&T Bell Laboratories, said it this way:

We live in a world where getting people's attention is the single, most valuable thing. There's information all over the place, but the difficult thing is to get it.

As a consultant, how can you get the prospective client's attention? How can they learn that you exist, and that you have something of great value to offer?

****

There are two basic marketing methods: indirect and direct. We'll examine how you can put them to work to build your practice.

I presume that you're going to want to open your own shop and be your own boss. As you know, this is what I've done, and I can speak with authority about it.

> When clients invest in consultants, they search for one thing.
> They purchase credibility.

To gain entry to a client's firm, you need to be perceived as an appropriate source of help, and as a nonthreat.

To appear this way, you should devise a solid marketing story.

Who are you? What brought you to the prospect's door? And what can you do for them? Furthermore, why should they believe you?

For instance, when I started out, I decided I would consult in the area of telephone effectiveness. I felt it was an underserved market, and I had, as you know, special skills on the phones and in managing phone operations.

I developed certain promotional themes. Here is a sampler:

1. Many people are offensive on the phone, without intending to be.

2. Companies lose customers, money, and countless opportunities, because of poor phone skills.

3. The telephone is a cheap alternative to face-to-face customer contact and sales.

4. Telephone effectiveness can be learned, and I can teach it.

I've heard that if you have a good business idea, you should be able to write it in a phrase on the back of a business card. It should be explainable and intelligible, immediately.

If someone asks, What do you do?, you can respond with the equivalent of my announcement:

> I show salespeople and customer service reps how
> to be more effective over the telephone.

When I prepared myself with this sort of "sound bite," I would often evoke this response:

> Gee, we could use some of that, around here!

It hit home. And that's just what you want to be able to do, because you're going to be called upon to tell your story, through various methods, over and over again.

Your personal achievements are critical to making your marketing story credible. By the time I opened my practice in 1978, I could already point out to prospects that I had nearly ten years of telephone experience; three degrees in communications, including a Ph.D.; and four years of university teaching experience.

So I positioned myself as an expert because I blended solid telephone experience with behavioral research. This helped me to say I was a doer and a thinker.

Admittedly, I began my practice with a marketing story that made sense. This was partly by design, because I was preparing myself for this field for some time.

What if you don't have the same opportunity? Or, what if your academic credentials aren't so numerous, or are nonexistent? Are you going to have a rough time establishing yourself?

Not necessarily. You should play to your strengths. For instance, I met a fellow who was an un-degreed senior vice president of a financial firm for fifteen years. He had worked his way through the ranks, and he wanted to become president, but that office wasn't available.

So he retired and launched a consulting practice. As an operations veteran, he could spend very little time examining the work flow in a complex business and offer meaningful advice, nearly on the spot.

Did he have a tough time getting clients? No, because he emphasized his strong work experience. The glamorous name of his former company also appealed to prospects. These elements were powerful enough to open some important doors.

There is a simple way to develop your marketing story. For the most part, consultants are hired because they help others to increase profits. This will happen by cutting costs, increasing sales, or some combination of the two.

What will your focus be? How will you help firms to make money, or to save money?

Once you have your story down, you can work on disseminating it through formal and informal channels.

Indirect Marketing

What makes something a direct versus an indirect method of marketing? Often, it has to do with whether prospects feel they're coming to you, or you seem to be reaching out to them.

I write extensively for sales and service periodicals, as well as for Internet publications. Ostensibly, I'm writing for the purpose of conveying information about my subject. Readers expect to learn something, and they do.

At the end of my columns, there is a blurb about who I am, and my company name and location. Sometimes my 800 number or mailing address will appear as well.

I don't pay to have my articles appear in these publications. But prospects discover me, and they have a chance to learn about some of my ideas and methods through them.

So for every article that appears, I'll usually receive one or two phone calls from folks who want more information about my newsletter, tapes, books, or consulting.

They don't perceive they're being sold by the article they've read. But one of its purposes is to bring people's attention to my existence.

This is indirect marketing. And most consultants would claim that it works very well. When they use it, they don't have to feel that they're carnival barkers, loudly hooking customers on consulting deals.

Indirect methods feel dignified, and they generally induce customers to come to us. This gives clients the very important feeling that they're choosing to buy, instead of forcibly being sold.

Direct Marketing

A direct marketing approach, by comparison, could include conventional advertising. Andersen Consulting, one of the world's largest consulting companies, started purchasing television ads a few years ago. It also supports public television, and it receives favorable positioning through announcement ads that are placed at the beginning or ending of programs.

Direct mail is often used by consulting companies of all sizes. Letters to top executives contain basic historical information about a company, along with a partial client list, and some brief discussion of consulting specialties.

There is also telemarketing as a direct method. Let's explore in some detail how you can exploit both direct as well as indirect methods.

Publicity

In mentioning the articles I write for various publications, I was describing one major way that publicity can help you to gain visibility.

Let me share with you some pointers for becoming a masterful self-publicist.

1. **Appreciate that most news is manufactured.** It doesn't just happen. Trade and professional publications don't have bands of roving reporters who are keen on making you the next consulting sensation.

They're strapped for personnel and money. Generally, they want two things, advertising revenue and a steady stream of editorial content that will attract a large and loyal readership.

You may not be able to help them with ad dollars, at least directly. But you can assist on the editorial side by funneling good stories and story ideas to the editors.

If the news is a manufactured product, think of what you can provide them as an essential raw component.

2. **The root-term in news is *new*.** How is your consulting work new and distinctive? What novel ideas or techniques are you employing? These are valued.

> The press also loves predictions, because they point to a new, and otherwise uncertain, future.

The sharp angle is the one that is noticed by jaded, weary editors, more than anything else. My very first press release, which was picked up by numerous newspapers in Indiana, was:

Goodman Gets Offenders Off the Hook!

This was the lead, or the headline, of my release, and many papers used it just as I had written it. The line was a teaser. It implied that I was someone who was getting criminals released.

The story was about how I trained people to be effective on the phones, and the hook ended up being the telephone hook.

The headline made people want to read the rest of the story, and that's what a good article or press release will do.

3. **Editors are like the rest of us.** Editors feel they're doing you a big favor simply to consider running a story about you. And they are!

So the worst thing we can do is to force one to work hard on our behalf. We should make it easy for them to discover and to celebrate us.

This is one reason some consultants employ publicists to package them. Publicity professionals often have newspaper and magazine experience, so they know how editors think.

My approach is to provide complete articles to editors, instead of simple news releases. Let me distinguish them for you.

The news release could be as follows:

News Release

The Telephone Effectiveness Institute will be launching its spring course offerings from May 9 to 16, with a national tour.

Two one-day seminars are scheduled for Chicago, Boston, and Anaheim.

Monitoring, Measuring, and Managing Phone Work is designed for managers of sales, telemarketing, and customer service.

Multi-Style Telemarketing is geared to helping salespeople, telemarketers, and even nonsalespeople to identify the most suitable selling style for themselves, their products, and their customers.

Programs will be conducted by Dr. Gary S. Goodman, best-selling author, consultant, and attorney. For
information, please call: 1-800-451-TELL.

The key to the effective release is to quickly address the
questions who, what, when, where, and why. Releases aren't
jazzy. They're bland and matter-of-fact.

When I schedule seminars, I send releases along with actual
articles.

For instance, when promoting the Monitoring seminar,
mentioned above, I included the following article, which I wrote
in 1995.

Ten Requirements for Measuring
Telephone Effectiveness

Phone work is important to every successful organization. Yet one of the areas that has been underde-
veloped in recent years has been the measurement of
telephone effectiveness.

Most modern phone centers, which are technolog-
ically sophisticated, are still very primitive in their
communication measurement techniques.

Certainly, they have machine-derived data about
a rep's telephone time on and off of calls, as well as average call length. But they have very unreliable information about a given rep's telephone effectiveness or
communicative quality.

The typical approach to assessing call quality is
the use of checklists by supervisors. These lists are
usually concerned with whether a rep said something.
This kind of presence-or-absence determination is one
of the most superficial ways of measuring any phenomenon.

Imagine watching your television news and hearing the meteorologist declare, "Yes, we had weather
today!" Of course, we had weather, but what kind of
weather was it, how does it compare to yesterday's,
and what is the prediction for tomorrow?

To get this kind of quantitative and qualitative report requires precise language and a meaningful use of mathematics. To say, "It rained today" doesn't tell us whether the rain was normal, above average, or below average. Tell us it rained four inches today and we have knowledge that is much more meaningful.

This analogy illustrates two of the requirements for measuring phone work. We need:

1. **Clear categories** and

2. **Quantification of data** to make it meaningful.

There are several other criteria that phone measures need to live up to, in order to be meaningful and to improve telephone performance and customer outcomes.

3. Telephone communication categories need to be **operationally defined.** For instance, in defining articulation, we don't say it is being understandable to listeners. We define it as: The full-formation of words, so they are immediately comprehensible to a listener of reasonable sensibilities. This tells phone reps to form words fully; in other words, it prescribes a course of behavior that they can follow.

4. The categories need to be **exhaustive.** All meaningful events in conversations must be captured by our measures.

5. Each category must be **isomorphic.** Categories need to mean one thing, and only one thing, and not usurp another category's territory.

6. They need to be **flexible,** to allow for unusual telephone events.

7. They need to **seem fair** to phone workers.

8. The measures need to create **interjudge reliability.** They need to be usable by different managers with different experiential and educational backgrounds. These managers need to score the same conversations within a margin of difference of no more than 2 percent.

9. They need to be **tested and proven** across companies and across industries.

10. They need to relate to customer values and **improve customer sales and satisfaction** with greater reliability than the systems they replace.

We have been using a tool we developed for
measuring phone work that we call TEAMeasures,
which abbreviates Telephone Effectiveness Assessment Measures. This method meets these requirements, and it has created tremendous results where it
has been implemented. To date, approximately five
million phone calls have been governed by the
TEAMeasures method.

Our experience shows that managers can be so occupied with their present measurement method that
they fail to stop long enough to compare it to other
tools that are much more successful. To make the
TEAMeasures system accessible, we're doing a series
of seminars across the country called Monitoring,
Measuring, and Managing Phone Work. For more information, please call: 1-800-451-TELL.

**Dr. Gary S. Goodman is an author and consul-
tant as well as president of Goodman Communications and the Telephone Effectiveness Institute, in
Glendale, California. He is touring the country
with his new seminar, Monitoring, Measuring, and
Managing Phone Work. For information, please
call: 1-800-451-TELL.**

How's that for a think piece? This one article has been published numerous times, and it really serves several important
purposes:

1. It establishes me as a leader in the field. Every Tom,
Sally, and Harry can't make up the kind of content that's in the

essay. I'm trying to establish the touchstone that will authenticate all telephone effectiveness measurement devices.

2. It alerts telephone managers to the fact that there are some solid criteria through which measurement systems should be evaluated. They should infer from my list of criteria that the techniques they're using now fall short of fulfilling these criteria. The perceived gap between their current level of skill and that which I suggest is available should motivate the eager beavers to contact me to learn how they can close the gap.

3. My knowledge is organized. It is contained in an easily obtained format: public seminars. By the way, I ran across a neat book called *The Teaching of Thinking*. It set forth some of the criteria for evaluating whether someone is an expert.

Obviously, he or she knows more about a subject. She knows she knows more. She knows how to learn more, still. And what she knows is organized.

4. My seminars are nationwide. This sends the signal that I'm available to companies, everywhere. Moreover, it takes financial clout to run seminars on this sort of scale, so I must be successful, right?

5. There are several small touches that are worth noting. My title, Dr., appears at the top of the piece. That provides instant credibility. I refer to actual consulting projects, and their favorable results, within the article. The message should be communicated that: What this guy does, works!

How in the world would I ever be able to communicate these important messages to prospective clients if I used conventional advertising?

It would be very difficult, unless I purchased ad space and reprinted my article, so it would look like editorial copy! That's not a terrible idea, but it's costly, and the disclaimer, Paid Advertisement, would have to appear at the top of the piece.

And that would diminish the article's impact.

One of the powerful dimensions of articles is the fact that editors select them based upon their intrinsic worth, not based upon being paid to run them. Readers know the difference, and they imbue you with much more credibility if you seem like a certified authority. The press is one of the few institutions that can position you in that light.

Of course, we have been discussing writing articles as if their most important attribute was the appeal they have to readers of publications. There is an even more significant audience for them.

Multiplying the Impact of the Press You Get

Articles can be even more valuable if you make reprints out of them.

A reprint can be no more than a photocopy of the piece as it appeared when it was originally published. Or, it can be jazzed up, to appear even more impressive.

Many magazines offer reprint services. They'll take your article and make a separate printing of it to meet your requirements.

Need a hundred or a thousand copies? No sweat. They'll run off that number, and they'll generally look very professional. The cost? Usually a few dollars each.

Every consultant needs to have a portfolio that she can show to or send out to prospective clients. When you have reprints, they help to establish your credibility by showcasing your ideas in a professional context.

Frankly, articles contribute to your reputation and attractiveness. I happen to believe that clients are impressed with consultants who have had their ideas popularized by large forums.

There is a sense that the ideas that get published are mainstream, or will soon become mainstream, and that the consultant has invited the trial-by-fire that comes to people who make their notions public.

Clients can almost feel that the consultants have been pre-screened for them by the media. Journalists are reputed to be professional cynics, and if they endorse a consultant by publishing him, then he must be okay.

It's one thing to say that your ideas are great. It's much more impressive if you can get the media to say that.

Getting Publicity Involves Several Steps

If you want to develop a great set of press clippings that you can translate into reprints, you should be prepared to structure an ongoing campaign to accomplish this objective.

Here are the steps I've followed that work for me:

1. **Develop a good press list.** Gather the names, addresses, and phone numbers of critical news outlets. Who should be on your list?

It depends upon who you need to influence, and the media that they read or tune into.

2. **Concentrate on the media that will grow your business, and not your ego.** Let me offer a few examples of useful versus useless exposure.

About three years after establishing my consulting practice, I hired a publicist to contact the media and to arrange interviews. I wrote the releases and articles, and it was her job to get them placed.

If making me busy was her goal, she succeeded wildly. I probably did a hundred radio interviews, with stations around the world. My long-lost cousin heard me on WABC in New York. My wife's relatives listened intently as I was interviewed by KABC Talkradio in Los Angeles.

I did morning TV shows, where I talked about my books and my consulting practice.

I even earned a five-star interview rating from a major news service. How much business did all of this glamorous exposure get me? Very, very little. I signed up one chiropractor/vitamin guru who was much more trouble than he was worth.

I invested many, many days simply preparing for and conducting the interviews. Of course I wasn't paid to do them, and when you calculate the cost of my publicist and the fact that I couldn't consult when I was doing the media crush, it was an expensive undertaking.

My ego swelled. It was fun, speaking to millions of people around the world. But the cruel fact is that I was paying them to listen, and they weren't paying me back in the form of giving me consulting work.

3. **Ink sells consulting better than radio and TV.** As part of the media blitz, we also sent out press releases and articles to newspapers. This was definitely worthwhile.

I was interviewed by the *San Francisco Chronicle, Miami Herald,* and the *Philadelphia Inquirer.* All three resulted in major articles, which became excellent reprints.

The *Chronicle* piece actually brought me two lucrative clients, by itself.

Because of the locations of these newspapers, I was able to exploit their clout in different regions of the country. Whenever I'd get a lead in the South, I'd sent out a copy of the *Herald* article.

I'm confident you'll find that getting exposure in the written media is better than through radio or TV. It tends to be permanent, for one thing. People can tear it out of a publication, to read it later.

You'll also find that articles keep working for you months later. I've received consulting inquiries a full year after certain articles have run!

4. **Consider concentrating your efforts on the trade press or specialty media.** I decided to narrow my publicity efforts to the business press. Instead of shooting for a general release to appear in the news section of a daily paper, I targeted business editors.

Even more valuable was the decision I made to write primarily for the trade press. In my field, this consists of magazines and newsletters aimed at customer service, sales, and telemarketing people.

After all, much of my consulting is aimed at improving these occupations, so why not put my ideas in the locations where they will be aimed at the right readers?

One of the very best examples of this exposure occurred when I persuaded a newsletter, aimed at salespeople, to write up a case study of one of my successful telemarketing programs.

I was interviewed for the piece, but much more important was the fact that my client was questioned about my methods

and results. The result was a two-page article that was glowing
in its praise, but it was grounded in actual, verifiable experience.

The article brought me, directly and indirectly, $151,000
worth of business. One firm read it, called me, and then sent two
people to a public seminar. That netted $1,100. The same firm
then purchased $25,000 worth of consulting services.

I used reprints of the article to persuade other clients to sign
up for approximately $125,000 of consulting. I'm sure the article
has worked even harder than this without my knowing it. I still
include it in promotional kits that I send to certain prospects.

5. **Commit yourself to having a continuous presence in the
media you target.** It's great to have a piece do well, and it doesn't
take that many first-class articles to help you to fill out a portfolio that will do its job in impressing prospects.

But, to make sure that you generate these gems requires
continuous mining of your media sources. I am committed to
having an ongoing presence in the trade press outlets I have selected.

I want my universe of consulting prospects to see my name frequently.
I should become brand-name to them.
And so can you.

This takes time and lots of exposures to accomplish, but it's
worth it.

So, how do I recommend you do it?

Commit yourself to producing news releases and articles on
a schedule. Write and send one out every week or two to the
twenty or thirty sources that you believe will help to establish
your career.

Because I publish a monthly Sales and Service Newsletter, I
write every day. Usually, in the morning, I'll pen 500 to 1,500
words.

I can easily write an article each day. During one recent period, I wrote 200 articles in a row, on 200 consecutive days. Each
week, I'd fax two to three new articles to my press list.

This has made me the most widely and frequently published consultant in the sales and service media. There are many side benefits to all of this visibility.

When editors are asked by readers who they recommend as consultants, I'm often on their short list. When I contact new editors, many of them have already heard of me, and they're happy to take my calls and consider my pieces for their publications.

So, the right kind of press can serve as an essential part of your overall marketing plan. There are some other indirect media that you should consider including as well.

Why Not Write a Book, While You're at It?

Very few authors grow rich based upon the royalty checks they receive.

But you can prosper immensely if you write a book as a consultant.

First, there is credibility. We've all heard the expression that someone "knew enough to write a book!" Well, prospective clients infer that you must know a lot if you have written a book.

It's one of the true marks of an expert. It can be a tremendous boost to a consultant's career if he has, or doesn't have, spectacular academic credentials to boast about. It certifies someone as being especially knowledgeable, and endows consultants with respectability.

Naturally, when a book is published, it is a great occasion to attract publicity. You can generate book reviews. Interviews are also easy to schedule if you have a new title to tout.

A book is also a great way to showcase your know-how in a very friendly intellectual medium. In a book, you can take your time to explicate your methods. You can calmly and thoroughly set forth why your methods are special, while others are so-so.

And people can come to enjoy learning with you. If you tell them how to contact you at the end of the book, they will.

Let me tell you how important this is.

I have written a number of best-sellers. One of them, *You Can Sell Anything by Telephone!* was read by a fellow in the state of Washington.

He was so enthusiastic about my ideas that he gave the

book to his sales manager. The sales manager called me. We met during his next visit to L.A., and he hired me to conduct an $80,000 project.

During the program, the president of the division popped into one of my seminars for about twenty minutes. About a year later, that president had become the CEO of another company.

He called me and asked me what I could do for them. The result was a $750,000 project. That work was especially successful, and after it concluded, the reference it provided helped me to be awarded with a $303,000 program at another firm.

So, one book reader made me over a million dollars!

I admit that this chain of events is rare, but I've landed many clients through my books. Even more readers have purchased my newsletter and audio seminars.

Books are the epitome of indirect marketing because they exist for their own sake, and not as some neon billboard that touts your services.

They can also be used like reprints, which are provided to prospects to showcase a consultant's ideas. I remember visiting a well-known company so they could learn more about my services.

While we were sitting around a conference table, I opened my briefcase and pulled out some of my books and fanned them out on the table. I mentioned that they could browse through them later, at their leisure.

They purchased a major program from me, so I guess it had a positive impact.

Volunteering and Networking as an Indirect Approach

A lot has been written over the years about the value of networking.

I would define networking as leveraging your acquaintances, friends, and associates so they'll introduce you to, or recommend you to, their acquaintances, friends, and associates.

It was once called referral marketing. Insurance agents and realtors have used it for years.

One of the ways to network is to volunteer your services to nonprofit associations. These can range from the Rotary or Optimist clubs to the Red Cross.

You can also join advisory boards for schools and colleges. By affiliating, you can get your name and your firm's name on literature that is widely disseminated. This is a form of free advertising, but it is better in the sense that it casts you in a benevolent light.

You'll be doing good for a worthy cause. People who have an affinity for the causes you're assisting may want to reward you with their business.

Some large consulting companies REQUIRE their associates to join a certain number of nonprofit organizations. It is believed that by doing so they'll bump into high-level corporate types who can help them to serve their firms.

From time to time, I've taken advantage of the networking process. When I was doing my advanced M.B.A. I became friends with the vice president of a financial company.

Before we graduated, he awarded me with a $35,000 contract. That assignment more than returned to me every penny that I had invested in the degree program, which was an expensive one!

Naturally, if you volunteer on behalf of a nonprofit, it is to be expected that you'll be given thank-you letters that can become valuable reprints in their own right. So others can learn of your righteous acts as well.

Indirect marketing techniques are often referred to as free. For instance, publicity is called free advertising. This is a misnomer that I would like to straighten out.

It takes time and effort to write articles or press releases. This translates into money, whether you're paying a publicist or if you do it yourself. The same intense effort that it takes to go the indirect route could be channeled into direct means.

It just depends upon your personality and where you think your effort will pay off. Let's turn our attention now to some direct marketing methods.

Selling: The Epitome of Direct Marketing

I have heard one marketing guru make this rosy statement:

> If you do a good enough job of (indirect) marketing,
> selling should become unnecessary.

The articles you write might attract just the right prospects, who throw their money at your feet while begging you to descend from your lofty perch and consult for them.

> It could happen!

But alas, not often enough to keep putting food on the table.

Selling becomes necessary if only to lend a degree of regularity to the consulting income cycles. We spoke about the feast-or-famine aspect to this line of work.

If you rely only upon indirect means of procuring business, you'll find your financial peaks are fewer and your valleys deeper. In other words, there will be much less time spent performing billable consulting activity than you need.

In a nutshell, you should never stop selling. Even if you have a client that is paying you big bucks today and you can see no end to the gravy train, realize there is one.

In fact, once you start to settle into a client's site, and your program is going well, the end is just around the corner. You're about to become history.

So let's focus upon devising a workable sales routine that can assure you a steady flow of business.

Mass Marketing Doesn't Sell Consulting

If you're used to working for a large company that super-sizes all of its sales and marketing activities, you can forget what they taught you.

Massive mailings or huge telephone prospecting campaigns are generally unlikely to work when touting consulting. Why?

Because consulting is an interpersonal communication activity. It requires intimacy and a lot of customizing. Clients need to feel that they are purchasing something that's highly individualized.

If you send out generic brochures to thousands of businesses, you're unlikely to get enough business back to pay for the mailing costs.

If you get on the phone and try to use what I call spray-and-pray techniques of persuasion upon senior executives, you'll encounter a similar fate.

You should consider highly focused direct marketing, instead. Let's look at the steps that are involved.

1. **Build or buy a list of suspects.** Suspects are people who you believe may have a need. Your supposition is based upon some facts that you have gathered.

For instance, when I devised my Telephone Effectiveness Workshop, I thought it would be valuable to businesses and well as to other organizations. Because I was nearly penniless, I decided to partner with colleges to bring my programs to the public.

I thought through the reasons colleges should be interested in sponsorship. My courses would be new. They'd fulfill specific and significant needs in the community. I had solid academic credentials. And we could price the courses reasonably.

On a conceptual level, colleges constituted a perfect list for me to contact. Finding them, along with their phone numbers, was easy. All I had to do was go to the library and look into a phone directory or a directory of schools.

2. **Devise your offer.** What are you selling? This is an important question to answer at each stage of the marketing process.

What can a customer be expected to buy, or to commit to, upon having an initial encounter with you, whether it is by phone or mail?

Most prospects need to be courted. They have to get to know you before they'll open their companies and treasuries to you.

So you're not going to go for the brass ring on your first contact with a potential client. Unless, of course, they express an urgent need, and the willingness to address it.

Your aim may be obtaining a solid appointment with them. What do I mean by solid? Solid means they are looking forward to your arrival. It also means that they're prepared with an open mind to hear what you have to say.

If they're clueless about why you're at their company, taking up their time, then it's Trouble in River City. On more than one occasion, I've visited prospects whose first words were, "So, why are we having this meeting?"

This question tells me that I, or my associates, didn't communicate sufficiently when scheduling the meeting. Of course, I'm prepared enough to answer it, but it is still disconcerting to hear.

So your first offer is to get together for a meeting. Assuming the initial meeting goes well, you'll have an important decision to make.

What's your next offer? And will you be on the clock, charging a professional fee for your exertions, or will you be internalizing its cost?

You might believe that the prospect is worthy enough to invest a substantial amount of time cultivating. It could be a firm that has a strong need, plentiful financial resources, and the sort of intellectual interest to you that you can't resist being attracted to.

If so, you might provide an extensive needs assessment at no charge. With other firms that aren't as worthy, you may insist upon billing for the needs assessment, which then becomes the subject matter of your sales offer.

So be clear as to what your offers are at any stage in the sales cycle, and communicate them to prospects as clearly as you can.

3. **Test your list.** I like to use the phone, as a general rule, to test a list. It's easier to make calls than to compose an attractive mailer, and you can generate instant feedback regarding your proposal.

I believe that if you're a good listener you can make a qualitative decision about your campaign after speaking to ten to twenty people.

I'm talking about communicating with people who can buy, and not with intermediaries, such as secretaries and assistants. If you have ten to twenty focused conversations about your offer, you'll be able to detect if you have something they want, or if your offer is inadequate.

You'd be amazed at how clear it is when you have an attractive appeal. Prospects will volunteer, "That sounds good!" or "I'd like to see something on that."

If they sound negative, or merely guarded in their feedback, you need to make some revisions.

4. **When you have a winning list, buy enough of it to facilitate a rollout of your direct marketing program.** It is helpful to market to a buying universe that is large enough to keep you busy.

You wouldn't want to get stuck marketing to a tiny market segment of just a few firms. Then you'd be a captive to them, and you wouldn't have much bargaining power.

So where can you look for lists? Start with the reference section of the town library. In larger cities, the main branch of the public library often has a substantial number of directories. You can also look into the collections at university libraries.

Look in the reference section for Bernard Klein's valuable book, *Guide to American Directories.* That will give you an idea of the great number of directories that aren't in your library, yet may be purchased from the publishers.

Libraries usually have state directories of manufacturing or service companies. They'll show the pertinent data about the company names, addresses, phone, and fax numbers.

The better directories of this type will offer the names of key officers. They'll also present approximate annual sales and employee counts. There will be geographical listings, so you can concentrate your efforts only in the areas you feel you can reach.

By examining the listings closely, you can zero in on the most promising firms. I know a marketing consultant who focuses on companies in the Cleveland area with sales between $5 and $15 million.

His theory is simple. He doesn't want to compete with the internal training departments at larger firms. The smaller firms don't have an elaborate human resources bureaucracy, and he feels he can penetrate them more efficiently.

By concentrating upon Cleveland, he says he can work in his own backyard, and avoid the hassles and downtime associated with traveling longer distances.

Directories are one of the cheapest sources of lists, because you can copy a limited number of entries, call them, and then decide whether you want to invest in the entire book. By the way, most directories are now available on diskettes, so you can enter the pertinent information into your personal computer and update the information it contains as you move through the list.

Diskettes are handy because they also facilitate efficient mailings.

List brokers can also help you to rent names, addresses, and in some cases, phone numbers. They can be found under the heading Mailing Lists in your telephone book.

They'll usually ask you who you're marketing to, and then they'll suggest certain sources that you can buy from. Magazines often rent their lists. If you know that your consulting prospects read a given publication, then getting that list is a smart investment to make.

The government developed a method of classifying companies based upon Standard Industrial Classification codes, known as SICs. If you want to market to all of the office cleaning companies in America, you can locate their code on the SIC list, and the list broker can then rent the entire known universe of those organizations, if you wish.

Or he can be more specific by renting only those names of companies with annual sales over $5 million that are located west of the Rockies.

A lot of time and energy can be invested in testing various lists. The minimum test usually involves a mailing size of five thousand names, and the cost of mailing labels is usually between $60 and $125 per thousand.

The most costly list I have invested in goes for $500 per thousand names. It turned out to be a big loser. Another one, in the $250 range, was excellent. As your lists become more specialized, they tend to cost more.

Let's say I want to sell my audio seminars by mail. They cost several hundred dollars. So, the best list I might get would have the names and addresses of people who have paid as much as that, or more, for educational programs of a similar nature.

There aren't many commercially available lists that fit the bill, and the ones that are available realize the value of what they're renting. So, they aren't cheap.

Obtaining lists is critical to your success as a consultant because you always need to know who you're going to prospect to next. You want to avoid wasting time in idleness because you haven't settled this issue.

Devise a Sales Routine

Selling shouldn't be performed in fits and starts. It should be a standard part of the consultant's daily or weekly routine. Let's put together a workable program for getting regular business.

1. **Select a day, or a specific time, to dedicate to telephone prospecting and appointment-setting.**
Some consultants earmark Mondays or Fridays for phone work. They'll begin their work at 9:00, take a short break at 10:15, and a lunch break at noon. They'll hit the phone again at 1:30, break at 2:45, and finish at 3:30 or 4:00.

From 4:00 to 5:30 or 6:00, they'll transmit any faxes they promised, or assemble the letters and other literature that they need to send.

There are other consultants who like to set aside a certain block of time every day, or three days per week for calling. They might make calls from 8:30 to 10:00 A.M.

You should try various routines, and then settle upon the one that makes the most sense for you and for your prospects. You may find that your prospects take long weekends, making Monday or Friday calls less productive than midweek efforts.

Remember, though, that your objective is to set aside the time that belongs to prospecting.

2. **Discipline yourself to make a specific number of contacts or appointments per hour or per calling shift.**

It's easy to procrastinate. There are lots of other things that may seem easier or more interesting to do than getting on the phone.

But you need to discipline yourself to set goals and then to reach them. There is a technique I use that can help.

I like to create a math of success. It's a simple process of breaking down my prospecting activities into a formula.

For instance, it may take me one hundred dials of the phone, during a given day, to reach thirty prospects. Of those thirty, twenty may express no interest.

That leaves ten prospects to whom I'll send or fax information. It'll take twenty-five dials to reach seven of the ten with a follow-up call within the week. Two of these folks will turn into a solid appointment.

So, one hundred dials, ten fax-outs or mail-outs, and approximately twenty-five follow-up dials will yield two appointments. Therefore, I have to prod myself into making those one hundred dials if I want to get two appointments.

If I want to see four prospects per week, I'll need to double that output.

This arithmetic doesn't contain hard numbers that are immutable. You might be utilizing such a great list, or your phone presentation may be so sharp, that your numbers will be much better than this.

Let me share with you an embarrassingly successful example.

When I launched my consulting business, I called colleges and asked them to sponsor my seminars. I had a teaching position at the time at DePauw University, so I had some credibility as I made my initial contacts.

But here's the killer: I sold an unbelievably high percentage of the schools I contacted. I made an initial contact, sent literature, and followed up with another call, about a week later.

Thirty-five universities sponsored my seminars. Fewer than five declined. In fact, I got so cocky that it came as an utter shock whenever a college expressed disinterest. One of the campuses of Purdue University said no, and I still chuckle about it, because every other Purdue campus, as well as Indiana University campus, said yes.

You don't know, as you read this, what the math will be for you, and there's no way to know until you begin making calls. When you find out, discipline yourself to pay the price of success by making the required number of contacts.

3. **Don't take rejection personally.** There is no reason to feel you've lost face if someone says no to your telephone approach. After all, unless you've used a video phone, they haven't even seen your face!

In the same vein, they aren't rejecting YOU, only your message, and maybe it's not even the message. It could be the medium of the phone itself.

Some prospects aren't comfortable meeting people for the first time by telephone. They might respond warmly if you were introduced face-to-face by a mutual friend or colleague.

But on the phone, they're cold fishes. So what? It isn't your job to warm up folks who are in a deep freeze. Just go on to the next person.

4. **Overcome your phone-fear two ways.** If experienced salespeople can be petrified about prospecting by phone, so can you.

But, you don't have to stay that way.

Phone-fear is to telecommunicating what stage fright is to public speaking. It is fear of failure. And it could be a form of situational shyness.

You can manage it. There are two ways:

(a) *Use systematic desensitization.* Force yourself to do more of whatever you fear than you ever thought you could withstand.

If you're afraid of heights, take elevators up and down, all day long.

If you're afraid of making calls, compel yourself to make one hundred of them within a single day. You'll find that you survive, and that the worst-case scenarios that you've victimized yourself with simply don't come true.

(b) *Visualize success.* Most of us resign ourselves to failure, and in doing so we produce that result. If you have stage fright, you can imagine dazzling audiences with your command of the language, your knowledge, and your wit.

Once you've seen yourself succeed in your mind, it's easier to do so in real life.

Managing, and ultimately mastering, your fears is one of the most rewarding growth experiences we can have as human beings. Don't deny yourself the opportunity of becoming a hero to yourself.

5. **Don't overthink the selling process.** One of my clients, the owner of an office machine company, said, "Selling is so easy, it's hard."

That sounds like a Yogi Berra-ism, doesn't it? But it's valid. Selling isn't an esoteric process. It could be as straightforward as:

I have widgets. Want some?

It's show-and-tell. Or, show-and-ask for the order.

Sometimes I think we do a disservice to people by making selling appear to be more complex than it needs to be.

One book I came across is called *127 Sales Closes That Work.* It certainly gets the point across that there are several different ways to induce customers to say yes.

Yet who can be expected to memorize 127 techniques for just one stage of the selling process? Could a human being be so rational that when she's embroiled in selling, she could seize the optimal close, in nanoseconds, from a list of 127?

No way. She'll do what I do, and what I urge you to do. She'll memorize two or three that are always useful, and she'll discard the rest.

We need to leave room for novelty and improvisation in our communications with customers. If we're overly technical in our approach to selling, we'll run the risk of becoming perfectionistic.

And that leads to procrastination, which results in diminished sales activity.

Let's turn to some ways to develop effective telephone presentations.

The Telephone Talk That
Launched a Thousand Seminars

I have mentioned at several points that I contacted colleges to cosponsor my seminars.

I decided before I made my first call that I'd use telemarketing, and my phone presentation would have to meet several requirements:

* It had to sound professional—not as if I were selling aluminum siding.
* It had to be brief. Because I was phoning senior college administrators, I couldn't talk their ears off.
* It had to be low-key and almost casual in its persuasion, and
* Prospects needed to participate in an egalitarian, two-way conversation. There had to be turn-taking and a polite balancing of speaking and listening.
* Prospects couldn't feel that they were being sold. They needed to feel that they were choosing to advance the relationship.
* I wanted to cover as much ground in a single call as was reasonably possible. (Remember, I was a college professor, not a full-time marketer!)

None of my prospects knew me, but they had heard of my university, so I would use that as a door opener.

I usually spoke to a dean's assistant:

Hello, this is Dr. Gary Goodman, from DePauw University. I'd like to speak to Dean Frisbee about a course that I've designed. Is he in?

I'd be put through, or I'd be told when he was due to return. Sometimes I'd set a telephone appointment with the assistant.

Would you please tell the dean that I'll try to call back after I've met my last class, at 4:00? Great. Bye.

Here is the text of my actual contact with the dean:

Hello, Dean Frisbee? It's Gary Goodman, from DePauw. How are you?

That's good. I'm an Assistant Professor of Communication and I've developed a one-day seminar called the Telephone Effectiveness Workshop. It teaches everyone, from secretaries to salespeople, how to make more effective use of the phone, and I was wondering how we might pursue the prospect of offering it through Indiana State.

That, my friend, was my pitch.
Let's analyze it, using the criteria I set forth above:

1. **Does it sound professional?** I think so, because it is very straightforward. I mention who I am, what I do, what course I've developed, who it's for, and what I want to know, right up front.

2. **Is it brief?** I think sixty-three words is very brief. The entire conversation, to the point that I've scripted it, takes less than thirty seconds.

3. **Is it low-key and casual in its persuasion?** Surely it is. What am I asking for? Am I asking for a COMMITMENT to conduct my program?

Heck, no. I ask how we might pursue the prospect of putting the course on. That's gentle persuasion. It seems as if I'm asking for guidance more than a sale. It's a very comfortable way of ingratiating oneself.

4. **Is this approach setting up an egalitarian, two-way conversation?** Definitely. By the time I've finished, it is clearly the dean's turn to hold forth or to ask me questions.

5. **The dean has the power to advance the relationship as much as he chooses,** based upon how much he reveals to me about the steps involved in running a program.

6. **Did I cover a lot of ground in thirty seconds or less?** I think so. My objective was clearly stated.

So, my mission was accomplished. But the rest of the call was equally interesting. I would ask the dean questions about how they promoted programs, and he would ask me about my financial requirements and meeting room arrangements. I'd also be asked if I had descriptive materials.

I'd promise to send the proper information, and then I'd ask a very important, reality-testing question:

You should be receiving that within two to three days, and assuming everything is in order, what will be the next step?

This was a critical, closing question. It got the deans to visualize a proper packet arriving, and to think beyond that point. They'd usually say,

Well, then I guess we'll select a date for running the program!

I'd respond with:

How much lead-time would you like to have?

They'd mention a certain number of months, and I'd suggest we tentatively reserve a date now, to make sure it was available.

We'd settle upon compensation, and then all that was left to do was to pop the packet into the mail, and follow up with a call to see if everything looked good.

Invariably it would, and we'd be off to the races.

This approach looks and feels easy, and it should. The best phone approaches are elegant in their simplicity.

One of the essential aspects of the presentation is what I have come to call a Perfect Question. A PQ does a number of things:

* It is enjoyable to answer;
* It arouses a sense of need in the listener; and
* It promotes self-persuasion within the listener.

When I asked deans how we might pursue the prospect of offering the class through their schools, I launched a PQ.

It was enjoyable to answer because it was polite. I didn't declare that they should offer the course. I asked how we might pursue the prospect of offering it. This is a gentle way of getting them to focus upon accepting the course, and most well-educated people appreciate the soft approach that these words represent.

When listeners heard the question begin with how we'd do the course, and not ask *whether* we could do it, they were set upon a path of accepting the course.

They had to be thinking, "Yes, I suppose we could use a class such as this," as a necessary precursor to even answering the question as I had constructed it.

By choosing the word "how," I built in the assumption that the course was worth doing and all that was left to decide was "when?"

Consultants solve problems. But first, we need to develop some common ground with the prospect so they will acknowledge and disclose that they have problems that are meaningful enough to jointly address.

This is where PQs come in. If we're on the phone, we need to briefly introduce ourselves and get people to freely state that they have a challenge that they would consider hiring us to work on.

One of my consulting areas, as you know, is telephone communication. Unless prospects believe there is a gap between existing and ideal phone practices in their firm, I won't have much of a chance to ply my trade.

So after introducing myself, I need to ask a few questions to establish that they are ready, willing, and able to hire me. I might ask:

How would you rate the telephone skills of your employees?

If the prospect came back and asked what I meant, I'd get more specific:

Would you say they're exceptionally good on the phone, or would you say they could be better?

If the prospect beamed back, "They're wonderful!," I wouldn't fight the response. I'd answer with:

That's wonderful. Have a great day! Bye.

Yes, the call would be over, because I would not have been able to establish the admission of a need. Please note that I am seeking the admission of a need.

Frankly, I believe 99.9 percent of companies need my help. I have tools that can make the best phone people, as well as their managers, achieve more.

But, if I can't get someone to freely admit she has a need, how will I ever get her to support and champion a consulting program on my behalf? Prospects need to be open and honest with consultants.

I realize that it isn't everyone's style to disclose organizational weaknesses to cold callers, but we need to touch a responsive nerve before we can justify investing additional time in developing a relationship with a prospect.

Here's what the best consulting prospects will tell you, early in your dealings with them:

1. They have a need.
2. It's important enough to address immediately.
3. And they would like your help in addressing it.

As far as I'm concerned, this is what a truly qualified consulting prospect will say. I realize that traditional salespeople believe that the most important determinant of whether a prospect is qualified is whether the person has the money to afford what's being sold.

Financial capability is less of an issue for the consultant than it is for the vacuum cleaner salesperson. Because consultants sell primarily to businesses, most prospects are used to making investments.

Our PQs are aimed at getting prospects to say they have a need, it's important, and they want your help.

With the phone skills question I offered as an example, the

ideal prospect would come back to me with a rating comment such as this:

How would I rate them? In my opinion, they could be a lot better.

I'd come back with:

In what ways?

That would elicit specifics about listening skills, conflict management ability, selling strategies, and so on.

I'd ask:

How important is it to your business for your people to be better on the phone?

Here, I'm trying to get the prospect to tell me not only that she has a need, but that it is significant to the proper functioning of the firm.

If I hear what I'm hoping to hear, that it's very important to customers, and to generating sales and repeat business, I then need to ask at least one more question:

If I could show you how to improve their capability through a customized training program, would you like to look into it?

I need a yes to this question because it's not enough that the prospect said that she had a need that was important. She needs to be open to receiving our help.

Some people like to bake the cake all by themselves. They, or their organizations, don't believe in using consultants. Years ago, Tom Peters called this mind-set the Not Invented Here syndrome.

Companies can become so insular and egotistical that they believe they have the talent and brainpower to solve all of their problems. They wonder, how could an outsider outperform an insider?

My final qualifying question, which I call a Desire For My Help question, usually gets them to say the coast is clear for you to enter their waters. Or, you'll hear the prospect say that you should stay out.

You might be thinking, isn't this a lot of information to try to get from an initial phone call? I don't think it's too much. You need to know where you stand before you invest additional time and money courting a prospect.

Let me give you an example of a wasteful way of performing the direct marketing process. This will help you to appreciate the method that I'm suggesting you use.

Most consultants who use the phones make numerous, but superficial calls. They announce who they are, possibly mentioning their area of consulting expertise, and then they ask if they can send some information to the prospect.

I would say that 80–90 percent of the people you contact will say "Sure, send it out." Are they telling you it's okay to go to the bother of word-processing a letter, packaging it attractively, and mailing it, because they're interested in your services?

Not at all.

It's their way of getting you off the phone and out of their lives.

Certainly, there may be the proverbial needle in a haystack—the person who actually feels a fairly strong need for a consultant's help. But let's say you've made one hundred phone contacts that resulted in eighty mailers.

Which person, among the eighty, is the real prospect? You'll have no way of knowing until you have called them all back.

And here is where most of the waste occurs. Do you realize how long it takes to apprehend a prospect who doesn't want to be caught?

I calculate that we waste, at a minimum, a full hour tracking and pursuing each dead-end prospect. So, if you carelessly mail or fax eighty transmissions, you're setting yourself up to waste seventy-nine hours with people who may have no interest at all.

Secretly, some consultants know that the marketing cycle becomes wasteful, but they persist nonetheless. How come?

Because activity of any kind can feel better than idleness. But it's wise to remember, we aren't in the activity or the phone call or the mailer business. We're in the results business.

And that's what our calls need to do: achieve tangible results.

I would prefer to have a prospect give me a sincere "no," any day, instead of an insincere "maybe."

With a "no," I waste no more time. With a "maybe," I'm encouraged with a false interest-signal.

So this is why we struggle to get clients to reveal their needs, to discuss their importance, and to invite our attention to these issues. When we have achieved an admission of interest, we can then direct our energy toward those who are most likely to buy.

I'm not going to bother teaching you methods for overcoming objections over the phone. I don't think I've ever sold a consulting project to a reluctant prospect.

And it's reluctant prospects that you would try to dazzle with glib answers to objections. Let me offer this tip.

A consulting relationship is like a marriage. If you have a tumultuous courtship, you'll probably have an even more tumultuous marriage.

So if a prospect says he's not interested, or if he tells you his company doesn't like consultants, don't turn him into a challenge that needs to be overcome.

Believe him, and go on to the next, more receptive prospect.

Setting Solid Appointments by Telephone

Let's say that you have elicited positive reactions to your PQs. What's the next step in handling the phone conversation?

Generally, you're going to want to advance the relationship, and one of the best ways to do this is by setting an appointment to meet with the prospect.

The idea of going for the appointment has a long and respected history in the annals of selling. One thing is clear.

If you spend too much time on the phone, you can overtalk. So, if the prospect is qualified, you want to get into the person's presence where you can develop some personal chemistry.

Once you're there, if your meeting goes well you might get

a tour of the facilities and be able to learn more about the company's circumstances.

So what's the best way to secure an appointment? I'll give you the language I use, and then I'll explain it:

There are a number of things we can do to improve your people's phone capabilities, and the best thing to do is to drop by, say hello, and get acquainted, and the calendar indicates a good time to visit will be Tuesday, at 10, or will Wednesday work out better for you?

This, by the way, is proven appointment-setting language. Why does it work as well as it does?

1. **We mention that there are solutions to the problems that our PQs have surfaced.** We're not going to get into them over the phone, because we don't want to get the prospect to precommit to one without knowing all of the details involved.

2. **Please notice the language that I use.** We're going to drop by, say hello, and get acquainted. Sounds friendly and nonthreatening, right? It shouldn't sound terribly formal, but instead, informal and easy.

3. **". . . and the calendar indicates . . ."** This is very important language. I avoid saying I'd like to stop by at a given time. By having the calendar do the talking, I'm more likely to persuade the other person's calendar to go along.

4. **". . . a good time will be . . ."** Not might be or could be, but WILL be. This is assertive language which is persuasive. Keep your tone light and nice when you use the *will* word.

5. **". . . Tuesday at 10, or will Wednesday work out better for you?"** This is a choice-close. It enables a prospect to say yes two different ways. It isn't a yes or no question that gives the person an easy out.

If you use this appointment-setting language, you should get twice as many appointments as the average consultant who asks for meetings by improvising his phone language.

Some Tips for Face-to-Face Selling

Let's assume that you've set the appointment, and you're ready to meet with the prospect. Here are some tips for handling the face-to-face selling situation.

1. **Be prepared to introduce who you are, and what your experience is, right up front.** This shouldn't be a long narration, but instead, just enough to tell the prospect what your focus is.

2. **If you can, prepare some basic questions that you can bring to the meeting.** The first kind that you should ask are circumstances questions.

I might begin with, "What kinds of phone calls do your salespeople make?" It's easy to answer, and it gets the prospect to tell me what she knows about their current calls.

A good question is also,

What sort of formal phone training have your people had?"

This will get them to smile, and to say,

I don't think they've had any!

If we're getting along, I might joke,

Does it show?

If they laugh at the gag, and say,

I'm afraid it does

they've actually expressed a need for formal training, which is exactly what I provide.

I might follow up with,

If you were to improve their performance in one or two areas, what would they be?

This gets us down to mechanics. I might hear, "They could be nicer," or "I'd like them to cross-sell some of our 1,001 items."

In a freely-flowing conversation, the consultant is like a therapist and a waiter. Through probing, we find out about our clients' unfulfilled agendas, hopes, and aspirations.

Then, when these needs are out on the table, we pull out our note pad and take their order for consulting, or for training and development.

It can be that straightforward.

3. **Just as your goal when you hit the phones was to set a solid appointment, your objective for the meeting is to advance to writing a proposal.**

I like to rehearse my clients before I submit a written proposal. I'll walk them through what I do, and why it's necessary to do it that way to produce peak results.

When they see a proposal a few days later, they won't wonder what a certain procedure is, or question its necessity.

4. **Make a champion out of your contact.** Most consulting is sold to large organizations. I encountered a statistic that said that over 90 percent of the consulting services that are used are purchased by Fortune 1000 companies.

In large organizations, few people can hire a consultant without obtaining authorization or at least a level of support from other people. You may never meet these decision makers, but your contact in the company will have to powwow with them and persuade them of the merit of your proposal.

They won't prevail if they present your proposal unenthusiastically. Getting them ego-involved in the success of your plan is your job, and it takes a first-class sales process to accomplish.

So time should be spent with your key contact or champion, as I label the person, to get him to identify with the program. Try to get him to tell you what a successful program will do for him and for his company.

Get him to visualize success, and to discuss with you what steps he'll need to take to get the program approved. Ask about obstacles that might be anticipated, and what you can do to help to make the buying process more efficient.

He might encourage you to meet with a few additional people before submitting your proposal. They could be the types of individuals who need to be enfranchised and consulted with before they'll endorse any program.

Although I have to admit that I prefer shorter courtships, and faster sales cycles, I've found that there are benefits in spreading out within an organization to develop support before a contract is approved.

Not only are you able to gain support for making the sale, but by getting various players' egos involved in the program in advance, you'll able to solicit their help later on to implement your recommendations and new techniques.

I've found that the average sales cycle to get a consulting contract takes between six and sixteen weeks. Ironically, it take no longer to have multiple meetings and to involve many people in the buying process.

The reason? You're doing what you'd be forcing your champion to do, by herself. And remember this: You'll probably be more thorough in selling the benefits of your program than a surrogate would be.

So develop a champion to run interference for you, but make sure that you are present to carry the ball across the goal line, if that's what the situation requires.

Crafting an Effective Sales Letter

There are circumstances when you'll want to send an introductory sales letter to a company, instead of making a phone call, or as a prelude to a call.

You may not feel you're great on the phone. Or you may feel that your consulting has to be sold at the highest possible levels and that presidents and CEOs aren't immediately accessible by phone.

Okay, let's write to them. You may find, as I have, that it's a lot easier to get a favorable response from some top executives if you approach them by letter instead of by phone.

A recent experience comes to mind. I was a fellow graduate student with someone who went on to become the president and CEO of a major firm. I decided to call him and to set an appointment to visit.

As a telephone expert, I'm embarrassed to say that I couldn't get him to take my calls. I stopped trying after three attempts.

I tried a different tack. I wrote him a one-page letter, accompanied by one of my national seminar tour brochures, and a few testimonial letters and articles. Within thirty days, the senior vice president, who seemed to be the second in command at the firm, called me.

We set up a meeting, and a relationship developed. I have to believe it was the letter and the accompanying materials that had succeeded where the phone calls had failed.

When we speak of sending a letter, of course I'm referring not simply to a single document. This is a packet, consisting of a letter, a biography perhaps, testimonials, and any other enclosures that you believe will establish your credibility in an attractive way.

What should you include and how should you structure the contents? Let's look at the cover letter and its requirements.

I look at letters as if they are spoken communications that have been written down.

If you begin with this premise, you'll create letters that will sound like lively conversation and not like stuffy, standoffish announcements.

It's tempting to become ensnared in a formality trap when you write. Most of us took English composition classes that stressed structure while discouraging informality. So there is a ceremonial stiffness and self-consciousness that accompanies many business letters.

I believe the best prose for business is friendly and straightforward and communicates from the point of view of the reader.

You might have noticed that some of the best letters, ads, and other forms of communication begin with a certain word.

You can probably guess what that word is, can't you?

You've got it!

It's *you!*

I've may have overdone it here, just to get your attention, but the *you* word is a delight to hear, if it is uttered in a nonaccusatory context.

One of my best-selling books is entitled, *You Can Sell Anything By Telephone!* and I happen to believe that the first word in that title is a grabber. Unfortunately, when it comes to developing promotional materials and sales letters, we forget that *you* should come before *I*.

The typical introductory letter is geared to introducing ourselves to strangers. So it seems logical to begin by telling them all about who we are.

But there's a problem with an egocentric opener. Why would a person want to hear about us until he knows what's in it for him? Let's put to work what we discussed about communicating with prospects by phone.

What's the initial thing we want to do over the phone? We want to establish a need. When phoning, we establish needs through questions and answers.

In a letter, we can also use questions to get readers to appreciate that they have needs. Of course, we have to assume what their reactions will be from that point, and build the remaining parts of our letters upon probable responses.

Recently, I revised one of my sales letters that sells my audio seminar, Monitoring, Measuring, and Managing Phone Work. I must admit that my initial letter was much too egocentric.

I wrote about myself and the product before going for the need, and my results weren't what I had hoped for. Then, I changed my opener, and the impact was much, much better.

This audio seminar is aimed, primarily, at customer service and telemarketing managers. They work very, very hard, and they don't win enough recognition or praise for what they do.

My revised opener sounded like this:

Dear Fellow Professional:

Are you and your phone people over-stressed and under-appreciated?

It's easy to feel that way. Like you're bailing water
out of a boat that keeps springing leaks.
Phone work doesn't have to be like this.

The letter goes on to explain who I am, and how I developed some especially effective techniques for lowering stress
while building customer satisfaction.
When I was doing a major consulting project for Xerox, I
asked some of the best salespeople in the computer division this
question:

Who are the best prospects?

I'll never forget the response I drew from one fellow. He
declared:

People in pain.

I asked him what he meant, and he said the best people to
sell are the ones who are uncomfortable with the way things are.
They want to make a change.
The role of the consultant who wants to sell his services is to
evoke that pain to get prospects to realize, in a supportive atmosphere, that they have a need that can be addressed.
That's what my stress question at the beginning of the letter
is all about. I know, from over twenty-five years of phone work,
that telecommunicating is exceedingly stressful. Workers burn
out all the time, leading to turnover and many other problems.
If someone can show them how to achieve more, while reducing their PAIN, he'll be rewarded with a sale. Using the revised
opener accomplishes this task, nicely.
Readers of the letter who aren't stressed by their work probably have no motivation to change. So they'll answer no to my
questions, and toss the mailer out.
But, most recipients will answer affirmatively, and this response will buy me more of their time. They'll think, "Okay, you
got my attention, now what are you selling?"
I believe a good opener will enable you to keep a person
reading for the better part of a page of copy. Within that page,

you need to tell a convincing story to hook them into investing more time with you.

I happen to be selling an audio seminar with this letter; however, the same principles apply to promoting a live seminar, or a consulting relationship. Let's look at the letter in detail, which doubles as an after-call fax:

Telephone Effectiveness Institute
631 West Broadway
Glendale, CA 91204
Phone: (800) 451-TELL; Fax: (818) 956-2242

✳✳✳✳✳✳✳✳✳✳

Re: Monitoring, Measuring, and Managing Phone Work™
A Special *Audioseminar* with Dr. Gary S. Goodman

Dear Warren:

Are you and your phone people over-stressed and under-appreciated?

It's easy to feel that way. Like you're bailing water out of a boat that keeps springing leaks.

Phone work doesn't have to be like this. I have developed a proven training program that puts the fun and effectiveness back into sales and service by phone. It's called Monitoring, Measuring, and Managing Phone Work™.

I know it can lower your stress and add to your joy. Before I get into how it works, and what the program consists of, I'd like to tell you how I formulated it.

I am a consultant to the Fortune 1000. One of these firms retained me to improve the performance of its customer service group of 100 people. You might be thinking, "Well, my department doesn't need any help."

They felt the same way, but they changed their minds when they saw what wonderful things they could achieve by making just a few, critical adjustments. For instance:

CSRs were measured based upon how long their calls lasted. This induced high levels of stress, because reps had no idea as to how to make calls shorter. They abbreviated calls by sounding short with customers. They discouraged questions. They even asked customers to call back if they felt their calls would last too long!

We developed a Call Path for CSRs that gave them control of conversations. It reduced call length by 10–15 percent, while increasing customer satisfaction.

Reps disrespected performance reviews, because they were shallow and they didn't point out their strengths and weaknesses in an objective, easily understood manner.

We developed a fair, clear, and participatory way of measuring the telephone effectiveness of CSRs. For the first time reps and managers could get a handle on call quality and know what to do, specifically, to improve performance.

Reps felt that they had no impact upon satisfying customers. Few callers gave enthusiastic praise to CSRs for their efforts.

We listened very, very closely to calls and we found that satisfied customers do three unconscious things that are reliable signs of their satisfaction. These behaviors are audible in all calls, long and short, standard and nonstandard. This discovery made it possible to measure customer satisfaction in an entirely new way that is better than old-fashioned and unreliable mailed-out surveys. (Researchers will tell you that unobtrusive measures are the best kind—that's what ours are. Customers don't know what we're measuring, so they can't hide their true feelings!) Reps could now listen for their "report cards" at the end of calls, and know exactly how well they performed.

I realize that what I'm saying may seem self-congratulatory. But we have concrete, external support for the fact that these new procedures work. Our client's industry customer service ratings went from twenty-four out of twenty-six, to number 1, within two years of implementing our techniques. This kind of result has been repeated at company after company where these improvements have been implemented.

Now, you can put these tools to use by ordering my ten-cassette audio seminar and seventy-page guidebook, *Monitoring, Measuring, and Managing Phone Work.*™

Here are some typical reactions to this information from other managers, who attended our "live" seminars:

"Outstanding presentation." M. H., National Pen.

"Great suggestions and ideas for monitoring, measuring, and managing phone work." S. O., IBM.

"This seminar gave me a link I felt was missing in our organization. A precise measure and tool for training and evaluation." M. S., Coca Cola.

"I enjoyed everything. The Call Path system seems like a simple, workable, and very successful approach to improving customer service." L. M., MBL Life Assurance.

How do participants compare this information to other sources?

"Top of my list." P.F., Berkeley College.

"Great, above the rest." S.K., IBM.

"Better." B. P., Berkeley College.

"Outstanding." M. H., National Pen.

"Compared to other programs, this one was more substantive. It provided a practical and useful program for monitoring and measuring performance." N. W., G.T. Global.

Here's what you and your staff will learn:

Monitoring, Measuring and Managing Phone Work™
-Contents-

Tape One: Managing the Message

Call Paths & Scripts; Methods for increasing quality, cutting costs, regulating conversations, assuring quality outcomes, enhancing supervision, instilling discipline, enhancing call efforts. Types of Call Paths: Intuitive; Key-Word; Partial Verbatim; Verbatim. Blueprints for customer satisfaction. The Universal Call Path: components. The three measurable reactions truly satisfied customers have. Why it's critical to trigger these customer outcomes. Managing the Three T's: Text, Tone, and Timing. Examples: the right way and the wrong way.

Tape Two: Managing the Message *[continued]*

How to send positive relationship messages to customers. The Call Path shortens calls by adding words at critical times. How to turn-take with customers to create a rewarding communication sequence. The goal of marketing is to create customer commitment. The goal of customer service is to create recommitment. How to get customers to pledge their loyalty. How Call Paths affect customer satisfaction and employee satisfaction. Five ways CSRs resist change. Peter Drucker's insight about changing habits. How some of the best improvements are counterintuitive.

Tape Three: Monitoring and Taping of Calls

How we learn the most from our calls. Practical and legal requirements of listening to and taping calls.

Why secret monitoring is usually ineffective and unlawful. How monitoring and taping further the aims of quality improvement programs. Identifying strengths, instead of detecting weaknesses, as the focus of monitoring and taping. Who should be in charge of the tapes and the recorder? Why reps don't change their habits when they're being observed. Privacy laws: what they allow and prohibit. Why violating the law is completely unnecessary. Penalties for violation. Beeptones, messages-in-cue, and their legal implications. The role of consent. How text, tone, and timing apply to customer notifications. Example: the text of a state's privacy statute. How often do customers object to being taped and monitored? How to avoid problems. An important legal update: *The State of Illinois vs. Herrington*. Its implications for your state.

Tape Four: Measuring Telephone Effectiveness

Phone work's importance to organizations. How measuring telephone effectiveness has developed. Telephone Effectiveness Assessment Measures (TEAMeasures)™: A new tool for evaluating call quality, rep capability, and customer satisfaction. Why electronically derived information about calls doesn't relate to real world of reps' calls. Ten requirements for measuring telephone effectiveness. How TEAMeasures™ operate. Who is trained. How TEAMeasures™ create a shared and meaningful vocabulary. How TEAMeasures™ relate to formal evaluations. How to measure essences and not appearances. How mailed-out customer surveys are inadequate in providing meaningful feedback about reps and customers. How courtesy and professionalism are misleading terms. Why customer satisfaction needs to be measured directly, within the four corners of calls. How to measure the Call Path.

Tapes Five and Six: Measuring Telephone Effectiveness

Example: The Jennifer call.

Exercise: Evaluating Jennifer's telephone effectiveness with TEAMeasures.

How to score customer satisfaction. Introducing Merit Pay into customer service and phone work. How you get what you measure. Suggestions for introducing a measurement system.

Tape Seven: Managing the Telephone Environment

What is the ideal range of temperature in a phone center? How to be sensitive to phone room moods.

Case Studies in Managing Human Factors:

* Telephone Communication Case #1

* The Bud Story: Portrait of a Troublesome Rep

Special Supplement: A Code of Behavior for Phone Centers

Tape Eight: Effective Management Practices

Providing effective feedback. Communicating honestly and directly. Encouraging openness and mistakes. Empowering reps to correct problems. Sustaining group morale. Reaching consensus with reps regarding performance. Negotiating performance objectives. Discussing evaluation factors. Using recognition, praise, and nonmonetary rewards to sustain and improve performance. Using objective measures of performance. How Supervisor Effectiveness Assessment Measures (SEAMeasures) work. How managers can be evaluated and evaluate themselves. SEAMeasures scales and definitions.

Tape Nine: Effective Management Practices

Setting high standards. Showing personal commitment. How can we improve this? Establishing specific
requirements. Delegating carefully. Clear-cut decisions. Building mutuality. Sharing objectives. Deadlines. Priorities. What is the most important thing to
do? Getting cooperation. Playing to strengths. Going
to bat for people. Reducing and avoiding employee
turnover.

Tape Ten: Special Challenges in Managing Phone Work

Recruiting and interviewing candidates for phone
work. Probationary versus permanent hiring. Balancing product, company, and phone skill knowledge in
the initial training process. Scaling telephone objectives to match rep capabilities. Compensating phone
workers in service, support, and telemarketing. Who
to hire. Extroverts, introverts, and others. Additional
resources.

ORDERING INFORMATION

Orders are accepted by mail, by phone, or by fax. Visa,
M/C, Amex. Address: TEI, 631 West Broadway, Glendale, CA 91204/ Phone: 1-800-451-TELL/Fax: (818)
956-2242. Checks should be made payable to: Telephone Effectiveness Institute.

**Price: $495, plus $15 shipping and handling. CA resi-
dents: please add $42.07 state tax.**

Let's look closely at some of the principles upon which this
letter is designed.

   1. **It's not short, and it doesn't have to be.** As a letter or a
fax, this runs about five pages. While being succinct is a plus,

you don't want to put brevity ahead of your goal to fully tell your story.

Remember this: You're writing for buyers, and not for non-buyers. People who should be interested in your products or services won't be put off by a detailed letter. In fact, they'll appreciate it.

Real buyers crave detail. The letter, especially if you're enabling someone to buy at the end, should be as self-sufficient as possible. That is why I've included a complete, topical outline that specifies what each tape covers.

2. **This letter appears to be selling audiocassettes, but it is also selling consulting and live seminars.** There are good reasons that I'm in the audio business. I think of audios as consulting in a can.

They're a huge plus for a consultant. One of the major problems consultants encounter is the fact that their income is limited by the time they can use to promote and to sell.

When you become product-ized, you break through the shackles of only having your time to sell. You're in the manufacturing business! It is a profit center, and it can also showcase your knowledge to consulting prospects.

Moreover, if you conduct public seminars, as I do, people who receive this letter may inquire about them, because they have been mentioned, prominently.

3. **The letter contains real testimonials.** I mentioned in an earlier section of this book that clients will rarely sing your praises if left to their own devices.

You need to actively solicit their praise and then transmute it into a usable form. Here's a little article that I wrote that explains the process:

May I Quote You On That?
by
Dr. Gary S. Goodman, 1995

You may have heard that word-of-mouth advertising is the best kind.

It is, but there's only one problem. Satisfied customers don't tell enough people about you. This presents a marketing challenge: How can we make our customers' satisfaction more widely known?

Try to turn their satisfaction into an endorsement. One of the best ways to do this is by obtaining an authorized quotation.

For instance, I was returning to a luncheon table during a break from one of my seminars when I overheard a participant praising my cassette tapes.

She exclaimed, just as I was entering earshot, "Gary's tapes doubled our sales!" Instantly, I asked her, "May I quote you on that?"

She said, "Sure." Immediately, I placed her fine testimonial into my national mailing piece. Our sales have increased.

Your customers are probably praising you all the time, not only directly but also to your associates. How many of these nuggets are being capitalized upon?

You don't have to wait for a quotable gem to jump into your hands. You can mine your customer base for them.

Call a number of recent buyers. Ask them what they think of the product. Often, you'll hear something right away that you can turn into a quote. Sometimes you may need to use a reflective question to put the polish on a quote.

For example, if you ask about your product's performance, a customer might say, somewhat flatly, "It works." You can probe further. "Have you had experience with other products of its type that haven't worked?"

Then, you might hear, "Yeah, I've tried everything!"

The trick is to pull together into a single, dynamite quote what has been said in fragments.

So, you've tried everything else, and this is the first widget to really work?

That's right.

"Great, may I quote you on that?" Your quote will now appear this way:

It's the only widget I've found that really works!

There are hidden benefits to mining for quotes. By getting customers to praise your product, you reinforce their original decision to buy, while predisposing them toward buying more from you in the future.

You'll also hear customers telling you how they're really using your product. It may be a surprise to you. This information can then be used to reposition your item by advertising new benefits.

So improve sales by multiplying the value of word-of-mouth advertising. Collect memorable and powerful quotations as a deliberate part of your marketing program.

4. **The letter is a letter, and not a brochure.** A final note about my audio seminar letter. It isn't a brochure.

I have tested slick, graphically rich brochures against dull, multipage, memo-formatted letters, and the results are a tie.

Brochures cost a lot more to produce, and sometimes more to mail, and they require long lead times to construct.

Letters are faster and cheaper, and in my experience, if you're selling consulting, seminars, and even audio products, fancy brochures don't outsell them.

So, choose the right tools to express your unique consulting personality and approach.

When it comes to marketing your services, your only limitation is your imagination. In the next chapter, I'll show you how to profitably package your knowledge as a consultant.

4

Packaging Your Know-How

*T*his chapter will provide you with various formats through which you can deliver consulting services.

When people think of consultants, they might see them as organizational therapists who listen intently for problems and then guide their patients back to financial health.

Certainly there are some consultants who operate this way. Much of their work takes the form of asking questions, analyzing responses, and setting forth recommendations.

If we were to sum up their objective, it is to discover what's lacking in a company, and then to suggest remedies. It's a focus upon what's missing, or not functioning as it should or could.

This model of consulting emphasizes interviewing, assessing, and reporting. And you can certainly work this way.

What you would be selling are three deliverables: a needs assessment, an analysis, and a report to management of your findings and recommendations.

For example, a company might retain me to assess the capabilities of its phone center personnel. Using a tool that I've developed, Telephone Effectiveness Assessment Measures (TEAMeasures™), I'd go into the organization and work through several stages.

I'd interview managers about their goals and problems. I'd meet with telephone personnel, and using (TEAMeasures™), I'd score their telephone effectiveness. I'd summarize the results, compare them to a performance baseline that I have developed at other companies, and then submit an oral or written report, or both.

To this point, my consulting would be descriptive, and then, prescriptive. I'd point out strengths and weaknesses; opportunities seized and missed.

In my report, I'd set forth recommendations for training and development to improve the effectiveness of the phone center personnel. I'd include suggestions for training and developing managers, as well.

Many consultants would stop at this stage of the work. They would be content to bill the client for the three steps mentioned above: interviewing, assessing, and reporting.

It would be up to clients to fix the problems themselves, through their internal human resources/training apparatus. Or, they could contract the work out to a second firm—one that specializes in phone training.

Why would consultants stop short of performing the needed repairs and enhancements? First, they might not feel competent as trainers. Second, they might dislike doing the hands-on work of promoting organizational change.

For instance, I was called in to formulate a telemarketing program for a manufacturer. After determining it was feasible, I undertook the development of the department.

I wrote the ads for the newspaper, screened resumes, and performed telephone interviews. I scheduled and performed on-site interviews, set compensation levels, and designed the actual telemarketing campaign. I hired and trained personnel.

I personally supervised the unit until it was profitable. Then, I interviewed and trained a manager to replace me.

It was intense. At one point, one of the original telemarketers had to be terminated because of poor performance. Guess who my clients wanted to handle it?

That's right, me! I handled it, but the employee was bitter, and in a huff, he grumbled about suing me or my client. It never happened. No self-respecting lawyer would have taken the case, because there was no case.

There are many people who simply don't want to do what has been graphically referred to as blood-and-guts consulting.

Typically, this is work that goes beyond the three stages I mentioned.

It moves into the rough and tumble realm of implementation.

I know a lot of college professors who moonlight as consultants, and they want nothing to do with work that thrusts upon them responsibility for producing tangible, measurable results. So their practices are restricted to the three stages.

Because I started my career as a telemarketer and manager, I enjoy having a hands-on approach. I've been there before, you might say.

I also get great satisfaction from having a permanent and meaningful impact upon the firms that retain me. In other words, I want to see my exertions pay off, big-time. This can't happen unless I involve myself in implementation.

Frankly, it's a burden for clients to try to implement programs on their own if I leave the details to them. When I do, especially in the telephone skills area, they normally underachieve.

I'm going to share with you my ideal design for consulting. Along the way, I'll explain why each step is necessary.

Before I do, however, I would like to tell you about some consulting formats that I avoid.

Hourly Retainers

As you know, from having read Chapter 1, I dislike billing on an hourly basis, from a financial point of view.

But, there are some other practical reasons for avoiding the hourly rate trap.

1. **Hourly billing encourages clients to be clock-watchers.** They rush you.

2. **Hourly billing encourages clients to compare you to others who bill that way:** plumbers, lawyers, accountants, and so on. And your rate could be higher than any of these practitioners.

3. **Hourly billing implies that the minimum unit of time**

someone could buy is a single hour. I don't like working in an atmosphere where I think I could get fired every sixty minutes. Five times per week is bad enough!

The CEO of a company called me to say he wanted to hire me for just one hour. What did he want? He expected me to evaluate whether he could successfully telemarket a product by phone.

Well, folks, that takes more than an hour to evaluate.

4. Even if it didn't take more than an hour of clock time, the consulting value involved is worth much more than what I could recover in a hour of billing. I simply must charge more money for that service.

Attorneys will often bill clients for two hours for a standard letter that their word processor can spit out in under five minutes.

"That's awful!" some might say. I'm not so sure. That lawyer has a paralegal or a secretary to pay. The lawyer has to pay the rent and the phone bill, and for all of the overhead items.

She has to pay for professional liability insurance, because her secretary could punch out the wrong letter, or do it after the legal deadline passes for getting it out.

And, of course, the lawyer has to use education and experience to determine whether a letter is the right step to take on behalf of the client, at that particular time. Or to decide whether a phone call would be better.

I could elaborate even more, as you might guess. A five-minute letter doesn't really involve only five minutes. And an hour's worth of consulting requires much more than an hour's worth of value.

By the way, I told the CEO that he'd have to buy a minimum of one day of my time. Based upon what he told me he was trying to sell, I had an initial hunch it would be tough to do by phone. He went ahead and tried to launch a program without my advice, and his company lost millions!

A single no from me, even if it had cost eight hours of billing, would have been a true bargain.

Avoid Contingency Compensation

We've all heard that top executives, such as Michael Eisner of Disney, have earned tons of money in contingency compensation.

And they have, usually from stock options. This is fine for employees who are offered such plans, and who can meaningfully control events so they can reach the brass ring.

For consultants, by and large, the reality is very different. We don't have any formal corporate authority. Our efforts are often diluted by, or blocked by, the companies or people whom we have been retained by to help.

So when it comes to engineering results on behalf of clients, we aren't masters of our own fate. If a prospect offers you a project that ties most, if not all, of your compensation to results, I would be extremely careful about accepting it.

How come? It is a sad fact that some people who think they don't have to pay something, won't. If they can find an out, they will.

Contingency compensation allows a very big out for the ruthless. Let me give you an example.

As you know, I have conducted seminars through universities. Most of them have offered me a speaking fee, reimbursement for travel and handouts, and a certain bonus for enrollments that exceed a number we agree upon in advance.

By the way, I recommend this sort of scheme because it assures you of some income for your exertions. There is a set fee, plus variable compensation that kicks in after a minimum of success has been achieved.

A few cunning colleges have tried to offer me a percentage of *net* proceeds. This means they take out all of their costs, plus their own fees, and what remains is the net. Then I would get, say, 35–50 percent of that.

When I'd ask what deductions they would make for their expenses, I found they were throwing everything into the mix. Secretarial charges, rent, phones, supplies—and this is just part of the list.

Had I accepted this as a typical arrangement, I would have been out of business in a flash.

The fundamental problem with contingency compensation is that you don't control enough critical variables.

You have to depend upon luck, honesty, and, above all, a client's cooperation in order to collect the pot of gold at the end of the rainbow.

For my tastes, this involves too many risks.

I look at it this way.

If I wanted to take on a client's business risks, I'd go into the client's business directly, and abandon consulting!

✸✸✸✸✸✸✸✸✸✸

Let me share another example of contingency compensation that went sour. A client of mine was himself a consultant. He had been a Yellow Pages salesman for many years before launching a consultancy that told advertisers how to save money on their Yellow Pages ads.

He'd show them how to design their ads so they had greater eye appeal while utilizing less space. He tried to sell his service on a contingency basis whereby he'd charge a percentage of what he was saving his clients as his fee.

He found that most of the clients who took him up on his offer were flaky. They wanted the service, but they didn't want to be on the hook to pay a percentage of savings.

The legitimate clients wanted to pay him a flat, one-time fee for his service, and then wanted to feel free to use the cost-cutting techniques he had given them as they thought appropriate.

So he was forced back into using a fee-for-service billing structure.

Some clients will bring you bizarre deals that even lawyers can't figure out. I'd simply avoid them.

Winning Methods for Packaging Your Knowledge

I'm going to share with you what I have found to be the best formulas for generating income, while addressing some of the built-in problems of consulting economics.

First, I believe that advice should be packaged into various delivery mechanisms: consulting, training, audio and video tapes, workbooks, articles, conventional books, and newsletters.

If you're able to diversify your consulting modalities, you can produce several income streams and leverage your know-how and your time. If you get stuck performing only on-the-clock consulting, you'll be caught in the feast-or-famine cycle I discussed in Chapter 1.

After taking many courses with Peter Drucker, he asked me how I was doing in my consulting practice with this question:

Have you multiplied yourself yet?

This question vexed me. How can a consultant multiply him- or herself? By hiring other people? I do that from time to time, but I prefer being a one-man band.

What are the other ways? Through products and by publishing. At least, that seems to be the way Drucker has done it, and I have also benefited from expansion into these areas.

Let's look at what it takes to develop a product line as a consultant.

Establish a Consulting and Training Routine

I gave you a sketch of what I do as a consultant. Let me be more specific, and walk you through one of my soup-to-nuts programs.

There are several stages:

Needs Assessment

I'll agree to spend from one to three days at a client's site to perform management and employee interviews. I'll also observe, firsthand, the methods that people are using in their sales or service work.

The Needs Assessment will give me an idea as to which of my techniques will or won't work. How is this client like others? How is it unique? And are there any new routines or methods that I have to develop specifically for this situation?

Usually, I am compensated at my standard daily rate to perform this assessment. In very rare situations, I'll forgo compensation in order to gain wider access to the company, and to have a better chance of proposing a winning contract.

Written Proposal

Because consulting involves serious money, and because memories can fade, I urge you to put your agreements in writing.

This doesn't mean that you can't form a valid and enforceable contract without a written record, because you can. From a psychological point of view, it makes sense to write it out.

If people see a written document, or if they sign one, they realize they're entering into an obligation. They're committing to a course of action, as well as taking on certain responsibilities for seeing it through or for paying off the contract price if they fail to see it through.

I have almost always preferred a short letter of agreement. I say almost, because there was a time after I became an attorney that I became formal and ornate in my contracts. I've mellowed, and I prefer using everyday language to spell out what I'm going to do and what the client is going to do; when and where it will happen; what the compensation will be; and when it will be paid.

I do suggest you make provision for progress payments. Let's say that my project is going to take place over six months. I may provide for three progress payments: a third up-front, before I begin; a third after two months; and a third after four months.

This means that the payments come before the work is performed. In the event the client breaches the contract, I'm not put into the position of chasing after my money.

If you allow the client to turn the tables on you, you'll get into trouble sooner or later. Imagine the client holding all of his money as you perform. He has an incentive to stall in making payments because he calculates that you're already invested in the project, and you probably won't leave.

This is a very uncomfortable atmosphere in which to work. I'd avoid it.

In rare cases, you might be able to get much of your money, 50 percent or more, in advance. One of my clients had to spend his training budget before the end of the fiscal year, so he prepaid my fees for about six months. When that big, six-figure check arrived in the mail, I got a very warm feeling, I can tell you!

The Customizing Step

In my practice, I have to develop materials that fit the situation of specific clients. In telemarketing and customer service, I write telephone scripts aimed at making calls more productive.

I also have to develop case studies and other training materials to suit the situation. These activities can take a number of days to accomplish.

First-Level Seminars

Typically, I'll conduct a series of seminars for first-level employees. These will be for phone workers, and they usually focus on telemarketing or customer service.

They'll take place over two working days.

First-Level One-on-One Coaching

I mentioned earlier in this chapter that I often get involved in implementing my techniques. Well, this is the stage where that happens. I'll spend one-half day with each phone rep to help him or her to improve. This is when results really start to take place.

Management Seminars

I have to smile whenever I think of it, but managers take much longer to train than reps! No, they aren't dumb. They're surprisingly resistant to change.

This is one of the reasons that, as a general rule, I put reps through their training first. That way, I can earn credibility for the program by racking up some successes with reps and customers before I turn my attention to managers.

I may have to sell my programs on a top-down basis, but I frequently implement them bottom-up.

Management seminars often last three days.

Management One-on-One Coaching

I'll work with each manager for two to three days. They learn how to coach and counsel reps, utilizing my methods. They also learn how to sustain performance and carry on the program without my help.

Periodic Enhancements

One day per month, for a number of months to be agreed upon, can be scheduled to enhance the program.

****

This eight-step program is exceedingly thorough and necessary if my clients truly want to develop their effectiveness. The training process not only tells people why and how to improve, but it actually promotes improvement.

Moreover, because I'm on-site to perform coaching, I can determine how to adjust and amplify the program as we go, to make it even more effective.

A program for thirty people could take ninety consulting days, and be scheduled over a six- to eight-month period. My clients usually see an immediate payback on their investments.

Although I believe that the components of the program are crucial to promoting change, I also believe a company that makes a relatively long-term commitment, such as that which my programs require, does better because it is buying into an ambitious program.

It becomes ego-involved in its success. I like this kind of consulting because I can have a major impact, and I save myself many of the hassles of having to find numerous, but less committed clients, to fill my calendar.

Sigmund Freud shared with us one of my favorite statements. A bold patient asked Freud if it was harmful to the client that the good doctor charged patients for their psychotherapy sessions.

Freud responded:

If you don't pay, you don't get better.

That's the way I view consulting programs that require clients to undertake large financial commitments. The more they pay, the better they get.

Why is this? They don't want to see their company's money go down the drain, and a failure of great magnitude would hurt their careers.

So, when they invest more, they try harder. They even respect the process more. Let me give you an example of the principle in action.

I had a client who was looking into providing sales training for an elite group of marketing vice presidents. These men and women earned about $250,000 each, and they were a pampered bunch.

The client mentioned the name of a large training company that he was thinking of bringing in. It charged about $3,000 per day for classes, which lasted two days.

I knew of the company, for which I had done some contract training many years before. I mentioned to my client that the company used contract trainers, whom they paid only $200–$300 per day.

I asked him, "How much value could a low-paid trainer add to the skills of marketers who earn five times as much money?" This question played upon the old challenge, "If they're so smart, why aren't they rich?"

My contact, who was a snob, was incensed. It irked him that the training company would charge ten times what it cost to pay the trainers, and it also bothered him to know that the trainers were not themselves sharp salespeople or high-earning individuals.

He turned to me, asked what I could put together, and I ended up with a lucrative contract. He felt better doing business with someone who earned more money than those trainers earned.

The moral to the story is this: In seeking consultants, money expended takes on symbolic meanings. People like to feel they're getting the best.

So you can charge too little, and your proposed contracts can be too modest to summon respect. Robert Schuller, the pastor at the Crystal Cathedral in Garden Grove, California, says that big projects have a better chance of succeeding than small ones. People like to be part of something ambitious and important. It excites them.

My eight-step consulting plan moves from the general to the very specific. I do nothing short of intervening into and managing what people say over the phone, how they say it, and when they say it. By being this prescriptive and hands-on, I can really produce great results.

You may choose a format that has different steps, but whatever you do, make sure to have a standard protocol for consulting. It will give you self-confidence, and it will comfort clients. They have a high need for structure, and you may not get to square one unless you seem to really know where you're headed, when you'll arrive, and what you'll accomplish once you get there.

Other Valuable Consulting Modalities

I've mentioned that I write books and articles, and they bring clients my way. These media are consulting conduits because we can package and sell information through them.

There are others that I want to share with you, because I use them and they work.

Public Seminars

Public seminars have been very, very good to me! Seriously, they've been excellent means for delivering information and drumming up clients.

Let's look at how they work.

First, they package a certain amount of your knowledge and make it accessible to a large number of people at once. This is a huge marketing plus, because prospects get a chance to try out your ideas before they buy your customized consulting services.

If they're impressed with you, and they feel you've helped them, they'll be likely to want to bring you into their companies. Because you're speaking to numbers of people at once, you're saving time.

It would take forever to have separate conversations with them, and it would be a waste.

There are at least two ways to put on public seminars: through self-sponsorship, or through an alliance. When you self-sponsor, you have to hassle with every detail of promotion, meeting room rentals, registrations, and so on.

I self-sponsor, but it takes a lot of resources to do well. When you make an alliance, as I did with colleges at the beginning of my consulting career, you avoid many headaches.

They're in the business of putting on programs. They have people who are dedicated to designing and mailing catalogs, handling inquiries and registrations, and making sure that there are doughnuts and coffee in the meeting room at 7:30 in the morning.

They add prestige, as well. Being sponsored by the University of Chicago means a lot more than being sponsored by the Flubber Group. So, there are many people who will imbue you and your program with credibility in an alliance situation.

And you are likely to earn some money for your speaking services if you work through colleges. But you can't use the forum as an obvious self-promotional tool. The seminar can't seem like it is one big infomercial.

Attendees will be furious, and the college won't have anything to do with you in the future.

If it seems as if I'm painting a rosy picture of alliances, I am. They can be quite beneficial. But there are negatives to be considered as well.

If you work through colleges, and your seminar is a big hit, that should be good news, right? It doesn't work like that. Sometimes, it's a problem.

I did my program through a well-known university. It wanted to fudge on paying my fee, after enrollments unexpectedly surged. I had arranged a bonus if they went above a certain number.

They ended up declining to offer my program again, with me at the helm. Instead, when they promoted it again they used one of their own professors to teach my outline.

In the thinking of the university, it owns the classes it offers. If you're a consultant, you have no equity. If they want to find another teacher to run your class, they will, and you'll be out.

Here's the problem with alliances: They're undependable!

Even if you win, you can lose, because of jealousy or greed, or a personnel change at the institution you're dealing with. But, they do help you to get valuable exposure.

Colleges, for instance, may send out a hundred thousand catalogs to promote their fall, spring, or summer course offerings. If you're simply mentioned by name, people can contact you about consulting.

How much would it cost you to send out 100,000 of your own mailers? A single sheet inside an envelope would have to exceed $50,000!

So there's real value in the advertising. Moreover, if you write a press release that the public relations department of the university sends to the press, you could get additional publicity. When I was a college professor, just launching my consultancy, I worked with the university to get my releases out. It helped my seminar registrations.

Of course, if you're persuasive, you might get the sponsor to design a special mailer to promote your class. This is great, because you can make reprints of it to use when you promote your services.

By tucking the brochures of colleges into your promotional packet, you seem to be certifying yourself as a smart consultant. Again, you're borrowing their credibility.

I realize that I've mentioned colleges a great deal because I've had so much experience with them. But I've also benefited from other alliances.

✳✳✳✳✳✳✳✳✳✳

You can arrange to offer your programs through chambers of commerce and local service clubs. If you develop your platform speaking skills, you can also get bookings before trade and professional associations.

I have a bit of a bias that I need to share with you. Generally, I avoid doing unpaid speeches. For instance, a large company that puts on conferences has been inviting me to speak before its audiences, which happen to be filled with fairly good consulting prospects.

But I won't speak for free, unless I'm performing for a charity. It's a funny phenomenon, but as a consultant I've found that:

> Free speeches beget more free speeches, and
> paid speeches beget paid speeches.

Tuck that little tidbit away and see if this isn't validated in your consulting career. I suppose it gets back to my point that people respect what they pay a lot for, and they look gift horses in the mouth.

A wise person once shared this bit of wisdom with me. He said:

Every deal must stand on its own!

Which means, don't give anything away, especially if you're a consultant. If you speak or train people for free, it won't increase their chances of hiring you for money. It'll lessen those chances.

So even if it is a nominal amount, I suggest you insist upon being paid something to speak. The fundamental difference between professional and amateurs, whether in athletics or in consulting, is that pro's are paid, and paid well.

Insist upon it.

Audiocassettes and Videocassettes

Another great way to package your consulting is in the form of audio and video programs.

They have the great advantage of bearing, generally, a lower price tag than consulting. And they can be manufactured quickly, in limitless quantities.

You'd be amazed at how easy it is to record audios. After I began doing seminars at colleges, I decided to develop a product that I could sell at the back of the room, after programs concluded.

I went into a college music department's listening room with a tape recorder that I had borrowed. Unit by unit, I simply performed my seminar into the machine.

I had a tape duplicating person remove the clicking noises from the tape that occurred when I started and stopped recording. He also duplicated about fifty or a hundred taped, word-processed cassette labels, and placed the tapes into clear, plastic enclosures.

And I was in business! I'm sure the whole process cost me less than a hundred dollars.

At first, I only charged $14.95 for a 120-minute tape. Within a short time I realized I had dramatically underpriced it.

I split the tape into two cassettes, and hiked the price to $199 for the set. That's right, I jumped it up over 1,300 percent!

I realized that I wasn't selling plastic. I was selling the training program and the techniques that the cassettes contained. My theory was that the tapes should be priced at a level that approximated what the "live" seminars cost. Public seminars had reached the $225 per day point, so $199 was a relative bargain.

I had seen a consultant advertise his seminars in the newspaper, and he made his tapes available in the same ad. I had lunch with him and I asked if it was worth it to advertise tapes that way. He said:

It pays for the ad!

That's all I needed to hear. Immediately, I encouraged my seminar sponsors to include my cassettes as an alternative purchase. One massive mailer got out late, and a large number of people purchased the tapes because they couldn't get to the programs.

That one snafu made me a lot of money, and I became convinced that having cassettes for sale was a very smart move for a consultant to make.

Of course, when you break into the cassette business, you're really getting into publishing. It's fun, and definitely empowering. It's a good business to be in.

I can publish as many or as few as I like, and my breakeven point is very low, because I keep my overhead down.

And the profit margins can be staggering. That two-cassette package that I referred to above cost me about $2 to manufacture. Recall, if you will, I charged one hundred times that amount!

I invest a lot more, today, on packaging and production costs, but the margins are still healthy. I urge you to put your ideas on cassettes.

Of course, you can do it without charging anything for them. My duplicator is trying to persuade me to use cassettes as the basis for a marketing campaign. His pitch to me is this: Instead of investing in glossy brochures, why not send out a free cassette along with a cover letter?

Prospects can hear your ideas, judge their quality, and invite you over for a visit to discuss consulting. Cassettes have been used for some time in the multilevel marketing world to garner distributors, so they might be useful in selling services as well.

From time to time I've sold videocassettes that have been made from my seminar appearances. They cost more to create than audios, so your margins will be lower as a general rule. But the same principles apply to them that I've mentioned with respect to audios.

Publish a Newsletter

A great way to package your ideas is in the form of a newsletter.

They're popular with prospects and clients because they can usually be read quickly. They cover a number of subjects, and you're able to showcase new products and services through them.

Publishing a newsletter makes you a member of the press, which has privileges.

I don't mean that you can get free passes to sporting events, but it might be worth a try!

A newsletter gives you access to high-level executives. You can interview them about their approaches to certain business challenges.

Being interviewed plays to their egos, and you can discover consulting opportunities that would be, otherwise, invisible to you.

Of course, you can charge for subscriptions. At this moment, my monthly Sales and Service Newsletter is priced at $122 per year.

It's eight pages long, and I usually insert six to eight major articles into it. It's good reading!

I allow other publications to reprint my articles, so I multiply my exposure before the audiences I want to reach. Occasionally, I'll assemble and edit my articles and spin off other publications from them.

Probably the best bang-for-the-buck that consultants can get from newsletters comes from comp-ing prospects with the publication. By distributing complimentary copies, you can assure that the right people will see your ideas.

If you actually have a paid subscriber list, as I do, this is truly giving your prospects an item that has value. Generally, they appreciate being on your comp-list, although you may never openly discuss it with them.

And seeing your ideas on a regular basis indoctrinates them. If they have a sales or service problem that calls for a consultant, are my readers going to call someone they know, or try to find a stranger?

Furthermore, I don't have to wait for them to come to me. I can send a few issues, say over a 90-day period, and then make a phone contact requesting an appointment. Having softened the resistance of prospects with the newsletter, I'll have a greater chance of opening doors and new accounts.

There are indirect benefits to having a newsletter. It keeps you busy, and it gives some continuity to your promotional efforts.

More important is the fact that it keeps you fresh, growing, and learning. If you have to publish your ideas on a regular basis, you're bound to do some original thinking.

You'll stretch, and stay informed.

Of course, it takes time, and a certain amount of resources, to produce a newsletter. I suggest you purchase a good computer with enough memory to enable you to load a number of programs that facilitate desktop publishing.

For about $400 to $500 in software investments, you can probably get underway in formatting a newsletter. Many programs, such as Aldus Pagemaker, have preformed newsletter templates into which you can insert your graphics and text.

To date, I have written 100 percent of my newsletter's content. This takes a considerable amount of time, despite the fact that I'm a fast writer. Choosing and arranging the pieces in a given issue takes time, and even if you use computers, it seems that a certain amount of cutting and pasting by hand is inevitable.

Then you need to get it to the printer. After that step, you need to fold it, put it in envelopes, affix postage, and mail it. You can outsource some of these functions, but your expenses will rise.

There are other ways to curtail the time it takes to go from an empty page to a finished newsletter product. You can solicit articles from other people. On several occasions, I have been asked to write for periodicals, and I'm usually pleased to oblige, because it gives me added exposure.

Typically, you don't have to pay anything to contributors besides giving them a free copy or two of the newsletter that they're in. The trick is to have enough sources continuously sending you material so you never run out of it.

Newsletters are, of course, instant reprints. You can fold them neatly into your promotional packets to be sent to consulting prospects. By carefully selecting those back issues that you think will hit home with specific companies, you can position yourself as just their kind of expert!

By editing or publishing a newsletter, you can also have something to boast about in your biography. It says that you're established in your field, and it confers a degree of power upon you. It's a lot like an advanced college degree, because it implies that you must be knowledgeable.

Given our society's continuing respect for the written word and for people of letters, you could do a lot worse than to publish your own periodical.

Internet and Other Technologies

The World Wide Web has great potential as a consulting-marketing medium.

Many of the print-related products that I've mentioned so far can be loaded onto the Net. I have successfully promoted my newsletter and other training products on the Net to a worldwide audience.

My articles appear on *Time* magazine's Internet site for businesses, as well as through other sites.

The Internet can be a low-cost device to get people to try your ideas. You can agree with other Net participants to link your pages to each other, thus encouraging browsers to find your material. If they like the initial information you provide, they can call, fax, or send an e-mail message to you to obtain more.

I think that 900 phone lines offer the consultant another medium for delivering services. One of the problems consultants have is giving too much free advice to prospects over the phone. Billing for phone consulting can be accomplished by credit card, but an easier way to accomplish this may be by using 900 numbers.

When you bill through a 900 number you can count on the phone company to accurately measure the length of calls. Because charges to customers appear on their phone bills, it is a convenient way for them to pay.

I have thought of linking 900 numbers to voice mail, so people could attend virtual seminars by dialing into my consultancy. The programs might be forty-five minutes to an hour.

One of my audio seminar distributors has taken ninety seconds of one of my cassettes and programmed it into his telephone menu for callers who want to try before they buy. He doesn't charge for the sample, which is largely my introduction to an audio series.

Consultants should always be on the lookout for new delivery mechanisms for their expertise. Advice and training can be effectively packaged and marketed through audios, videos, newsletters, telecommunications, and the Internet, as well as through traditional, face-to-face counseling.

In the next chapter, I'll share some secrets with you for how you can make a smooth and successful transition into an exciting consulting career.

5

Making the Transition Into Consulting

*T*he wise owner of a newspaper hired a business manager to take over control of the publication. His advice to the new chief:

There are probably a hundred ways to run this paper. All I ask is that you pick one, and stick to it!

I feel the same way about beginning your new life as a consultant.

There are lots of ways you can make the transition. Let me first speak about the things that might get in your way, before I explore some of the paths that are available for launching your new consulting practice.

Procrastination

Procrastination is the bad habit of putting off tasks until another time. Why do we procrastinate?

Many of us are stuck in habit patterns that are comfortable.

They seem predictable. By changing our lives, we upset the balance we used to count on.

Instead of embracing uncertainty as an exhilarating challenge, we opt for the known, and eschew the unknown.

In the movie *The Shawshank Redemption,* old-timers who are paroled from prison find that their new world of freedom is threatening. Some contemplate committing another crime so they can return to the security of the routine they used to count on, behind bars.

Fear of Failure

It is the rare individual who thinks of new endeavors with such supreme self-confidence that he always says, "I can do that!"

If you haven't run your own business before, becoming a consultant, where you're suddenly responsible for every detail of marketing and operations, can seem daunting.

Many of us look to the past to see if we are capable of meeting a present or future challenge. "Gee, I've never done that" can be a statement that we utter that has the effect of debilitating ourselves.

We can easily grow intimidated because we're afraid to fail.

You don't have to worry about failing, at least from the standpoint of handling the consulting process itself.

Most clients that you'll encounter have had very little experience with consultants. Frankly, there are very few standards that govern the profession, at least at this time.

Fear of failure is often a concern that we'll be negatively evaluated. Well, it's not likely that we'll be compared to other consultants, because many of us work in idiosyncratic ways.

This is one of the reasons that I like the field. I'm free to structure my practice around my strengths, which happen to be in written and spoken communications. Another consultant could look at the same client situation and choose to attack its challenges from a completely different perspective.

Does that mean that he's right and I'm wrong? Not at all. We simply have different views about how to get the job done.

In a few weeks, I'll be giving a speech at my alma mater,

Loyola Law School, on the subject of consulting as an alternative to the traditional legal career. One of the things I'm going to point out that distinguishes the law from consulting is that the practice of law is highly prescribed in how attorneys must do their work.

You have to meet external deadlines for filing cases and motions. You need to identify certain issues in fact patterns. If you overlook issues or strategies, you could easily be sanctioned for misconduct by the bar association, or even be sued for malpractice.

In consulting, there is no association that you must join that can excommunicate or disbar you. You can be sued for malpractice as a consultant, but it's unlikely because it would be difficult to establish that a standard of care that is widely accepted in the profession had been violated. There are many approaches to a consulting challenge.

Fundamentally, as a consultant you'll know more about your subject than your clients. That's why they'll hire you, and in most cases, that's why they'll defer to you. If they didn't sincerely believe you knew more, they wouldn't have hired you in the first place.

As you gain experience in consulting, you'll learn more about your area. And you'll add to your know-how in a more organized and efficient way than your clients. So failing will become less and less likely.

Take comfort in the fact that every surgeon had a very first patient!

Should You Quit Your Day Job?

Lots of consultants begin their second careers while they're moonlighting during their first. It's a good idea.

I was teaching college when a call came into my academic department from a medical association. Its members wanted training in public speaking so they could lobby against skyrocketing insurance premiums.

The chair of my department said they were willing to pay $25 per hour, which was very good money to me at the time. I formulated a class for them, and it was a success. By popular demand, I repeated it.

I also wrote speeches for political candidates. Most of these consulting engagements were short-term, but reasonably well paying. I enjoyed doing them.

And I didn't have to give up my day job. This is a safe way to get into consulting. When you have an external source of income, you really don't have to worry about immediately mastering the marketing side of consulting.

You don't have to solicit, or, for that matter, accept every offer that comes your way. You can be selective in the jobs you undertake. If you believe that there is an underexploited area, as I perceived in telephone communication, then you can afford to dabble in it without worrying about financial consequences.

When I ran my first Telephone Effectiveness Seminar at Cal State Los Angeles, there were no more than seven students who enrolled. From a financial standpoint, the program wasn't a huge hit. But it was a smash with the people who did attend. They liked it and were grateful that I had developed it.

It was their qualitative reaction to the course's content that told me I had a winner on my hands. The money, and wall-to-wall registrations in my courses, came later.

When you don't have pressing financial burdens, you can enjoy a degree of role distance from what you're experimenting with. In fact, you can think of consulting as just that—an experiment.

If one approach to it fails, so what? That's the price of progress. You can always keep tinkering until you find the right combination.

What if You're Chucking Your Day Job, or It Chucked You?

What if you don't have the luxury of testing the consulting waters before jumping in?

You may have lost your day job, or you may be tired of it. Or you might be the kind of person who likes to devote full-time attention to one career at a time.

How should you begin?

I suggest you plan a very focused sales and marketing campaign.

What Is the Number-One Benefit You're Promoting?

If you've read books on selling, you've probably come across the distinction between: features and benefits.

A feature is an aspect of a product. My station wagon has a turbodiesel engine. The benefits of the turbodiesel are durability, fuel economy, and adequate power when you need it.

Effective selling is a process of translating features into the kinds of benefits that customers value.

You're a consultant, so what are you selling? If you're assisting businesses, then you're selling profits.

There are two fundamental ways of increasing profits: (1) build sales or (2) cut costs.

Which are you going to promote as your specific purpose?

Let me give you an example from my consulting practice.

You already know that I offer seminars and one-on-one training in the areas of customer service, sales, and telemarketing. So, how do these activities (features) translate into profits (benefits)?

I could contact a list of prospects and say:

> I'm a telephone consultant and I'll show you how to improve sales and service by phone!

This is a valid statement, but it's flawed. What do you think is wrong with it?

It's vague.

I have been very successful saying this, however:

> I'm a telephone consultant and I'll show you how to make calls 10-15 percent shorter, but better. How might that help you?

Yesterday, I received a phone call from a company that has 3,500 people on the phones, full-time. That's 28,000 phone hours every day.

Each phone hour must cost them a minimum of twenty dollars. If I showed them how to reduce call length by 10 percent, they'd curtail 2,800 hours from conversations, and save $56,000 per day.

Given the number of people involved, it might require an investment in consulting of $250,000 or more. But the client would recoup the investment in a single week of savings!

It takes a lot of work and some very specialized knowledge that I've developed to reduce call length. But I do it.

So to earn consulting business, you should develop a specific deliverable. Ask yourself:

> What is the single, overriding benefit that I can deliver to clients that will make them enthusiastic about bringing me in?

Then, devise your entire sales and marketing campaign around that single theme.

Isn't that putting all of your eggs into one basket?

Not really. You don't have any eggs, right? You're starting from a dead stop. You need clients, ASAP, and you can't afford to fool around.

By marshaling your resources behind the most important deliverable, you assure yourself of one critical outcome:

Your marketing message will be clear, and it should be immediately understood.

That's a huge plus in a marketplace that bombards prospects with me-too messages from vendors who all seem to be alike. By focusing upon one essential benefit, you create something that every business person craves:

> Product differentiation.

You stand apart from the crowd. You're an entity unto yourself.

I don't know of any other consultant who can authoritatively promise and deliver shorter phone calls!

So on the marketing battlefield, I occupy the high ground. I am in a commanding position. I know my worth, and I can spell it out in dollars and cents for my clients.

How many people do you have on the phone? How much does a phone hour cost?

The answers to these simple questions will enable me to cost-justify my involvement with the company.

This is power. And money will flow in, once we make our specific contribution known.

Find the lever that is long and strong enough to move your prospects out of indifference. Find their pain. Then, promise to help.

You May Have to Volunteer

How can you get a job that requires experience if you've never had experience?

This is a riddle that confronts first-time job seekers as well as career changers. It can be tough getting that first consulting assignment.

People want to see credentials that point to your achievements before they start writing checks to pay for your purported expertise.

Who can blame them?

But, there is a way of getting vital consulting experience, with very little pressure to produce huge results. It is through volunteer work with deserving organizations.

Volunteering at this stage of your career is different than giving away free consulting. When you're starting out, you don't have a tried and true product yet. So, there hasn't been an economic value attached to your services that you can waive. Plus, you'll be getting something as valuable as money in return: experience and credentials.

You can volunteer anywhere. Most folks choose to do it at nonprofit organizations, but there is nothing to prevent you from working gratis at the most profitable company on earth.

Students do it all the time. They even have a special name and status. They're called interns.

There are some companies that I want to work with so much that I'll donate some of my up-front time with them. I'll give away my needs assessment so I can get inside to meet people and determine how to add value.

One organization, which was openly anticonsultant, opened its doors to me on this basis. I made about four visits to various sites. I interviewed employees and managers. I observed the work taking place.

The firm thought it was super-sharp when it came to phone skills. It had just purchased a training program for showing reps how to suggestively sell add-on products.

My research revealed that employees were distressed by the requirement to cross-sell, because they were measured based upon call length.

How could they add a lot of verbiage about other products without making calls longer?

That's where I came in. Aha! They had articulated a need that I was uniquely equipped to address!

So volunteering can help you to penetrate firms with which you want to develop a paying consulting relationship.

But you can also bolster your resume by working with non-profits. They really appreciate free labor. And they're usually more than happy to write letters of appreciation that you can use to impress your initial, paying clients.

By the way, ask them to substitute the word "working" for "volunteering" when they pen those lovely memos.

> Thanks, Bob, for all of your productive work here at the Heart Association. Your professional manner and unique knowledge helped us to increase donations by 60 percent.

When you think about it, whether you are paid or not says nothing about the quality of your work. If you helped, you helped.

Don't Position Yourself as a Generalist

Avoid trying to position yourself as an all-purpose fix-it person. There is an occupation for jacks of all trades. They're handymen and women, and they don't earn nearly as much as special-ists, such as plumbers and carpenters.

If you think about it, when you position yourself as a gener-alist you go into competition with everyone. Existing employees in companies think that they're generalists. So why should they hire you?

They'll bring you in if you know more than they do, *period.* They're not looking for clones when they retain consultants. They're looking for people who bring something specific and valuable to the table.

It's a Blessing if You Start Out Nearly Broke

Money can be a real hindrance to people who start their own consulting practices.

Just as my Ph.D. buddies did, they rent the fanciest space they can find, thinking this will impress clients. Remember this:

> Most clients will never see your office.
> So what does it matter if it is in a linen closet at home,
> or in the corner of the living room?

The fact is, you'll be visiting them much more frequently than they'll be visiting you. After all, what will they see if they stop by?

There you'll be, thinking. How dramatic! Or, you might be on the phone, or writing proposals. They'll be bored to tears and they'll just get in your way.

Anyway, a lot of your work will be done at their place of business, so your need for big square footage will be a figment of your ego.

A consulting office doesn't have to look a certain way. It simply needs to be functional.

I told you that I bought my own building. What I didn't say was how often I can be found there.

When I have brought in the biggest bucks, my property has looked like a ghost town. There have been months where I've spent less than three hours there.

Now that we have laptops (which I'm using to write these words) and cellular phones and modems, fixed offices are taking on less prominence as workplaces.

I would avoid taking on expenses, every step of the way, as you start consulting. Frankly, an office, unless it's dirt cheap and superconvenient, is a frill you can afford to forgo.

Should you have fancy cars and flashy jewelry to show off your success?

The clients who seem to be most impressed with your status symbols are the ones who are without them. When I've run training programs for certain groups of salespeople, they've complimented me on my taste in luxury cars.

One client, in the bond business, took a really close look at my Rolex, because he collected them. Other clients are very low-key, and they don't display wealth if they can avoid it.

I've consulted to millionaire investment advisors in small Illinois farm towns who wouldn't be caught dead driving a flashy car. In fact, they'll choose Oldsmobiles instead of Cadillacs to downplay their wealth.

Here are some things you should definitely invest in:

1. **High-quality letterhead and business cards.** Choose a heavy bond type of paper, with texture. This confers an impression of prestige, without shouting.

When you're recommending consulting ventures that involve big investments, you want to avoid looking cheap.

I made some major mistakes in overusing my fax machine. It's fine for selling certain items, but if you're marketing professional services, your image will suffer when it is spit out by a prospect's fax.

A prospect in the auto business urged me to fax a proposal to him by a certain time. I should have printed the proposal on my Laserwriter, and included a lot of supporting documents.

Instead, I rushed him a few pages from my laptop. We haven't had a friendly conversation since!

I don't like to use brochures to sell consulting. Reluctantly, I used them to pitch public seminars and products.

By nature, they're too generic, and very costly.

You might want to have a designer produce a customized

logo for your literature. If it's tasteful, it can convey a solid image of your firm.

2. **Buy yourself two or three great consulting outfits.** A crisp business look is very helpful to the consultant.

Only once have I heard a prospect criticize me for looking like a suit when I arrived in one of my London-tailored, double-breasteds. The critic was in his early twenties and immature.

I think super clothes can make a great statement. They imbue clients with confidence, and you walk taller when you're well-outfitted.

One client I had was located at the beach. It was a software firm whose founders were self-described hippies. I was told, immediately upon being retained, that you can lose the suit!

Naturally, I adjusted. The assignment spoiled me, because I could wear jeans and athletic shoes or boots, and take lunchtime walks near the sand and surf.

3. **Stick with a conventional briefcase.** Although I have a sturdy, over-the-shoulder, soft-sided Samsonite bag that is made to carry my laptop and tons of junk, it turns too many heads at client sites.

It looks as if I'm there for the weekend, instead of for business.

I've reverted to a no-nonsense briefcase. It's boring, but sturdy. And I keep it reasonably well-polished.

4. **Buy a portable cellular phone.** I tell most clients they can reach me nearly any time.

I have call forwarding on my cell phone, so I can be called by an L.A. client when I'm in Chicago. All they know is that the phone rings a few more times before they reach me.

Phones and pagers are tools that build client confidence. Knowing you're accessible is a great comfort.

If I seem very concerned about generating confidence in my abilities, I
am. Clients who doubt you can be a real pain.

Like insecure people in our personal lives, they constantly require reassurance. To even try the new techniques you'll recommend as a consultant, they need to believe they'll work.

I'm reluctant to compare consultants to witch doctors and faith healers, but there is a similarity!

Your patients will improve if they have a powerful belief in your magic, so we should assist this psychological phenomenon by providing symbols that engender confidence.

You May Need to Reposition Your Service Until You Succeed

One of the main tasks you'll face as a new consultant is to align your work products very carefully with the desires and buying habits of your target market.

It can take time to get it right, and once you think you have, the market shifts. Here's an example from my consultancy.

When I started my practice, I formulated a basic Telephone Effectiveness Seminar. It promised to be everything to everybody.

I advertised to salespeople as well as to secretaries. I had pointers for telephone etiquette and for sales together in the same program. I taught salespeople how to penetrate call screening that the secretaries sitting in adjacent seminar seats were trying to effectuate.

It was actually fun, putting these adversaries together in the same room. However, I noticed that evaluations mentioned that the secretaries could live without the sales stuff, and vice versa.

So I split the program into two courses: one aimed at customer service, and the other at selling. It worked, and I was able to double the number of seminar bookings that I had with colleges.

Had I not done this, someone else would have, and they would have taken the market away, or at least have penetrated my college distribution network.

By the early 1990s, telemarketing courses were everywhere. It wouldn't have done any good to have offered mine unless I differentiated it.

So I thought through where the general topic was vulnerable. I decided that telemarketing training failed because it made people sound as if they were robots who read mind-numbing pitches to hostile prospects.

This breeds rejection, and high employee turnover. So I developed a new way of telemarketing. In fact, I called it The New Telemarketing™.

I ran this seminar in some of the largest seminar markets: L.A./Orange County, San Francisco, Chicago, New York, and Houston.

It did well, and participants liked it.

I recorded an audiocassette seminar with the same name, which is very popular.

My concept behind the course was product differentiation and a repositioning of the telemarketing topic in the minds of people who were put off by traditional tele-selling practices.

By calling it a New Telemarketing™, I felt the title said it all. Forget the old. Here is the new and improved version. Plus, new would always distinguish my course as being leading edge.

Unfortunately, the class wasn't the huge hit I thought it deserved to be. From time to time, we'd get big enrollments in the sessions, and the consulting after-market was decent.

I took some time off from offering the class—about a year and a half. I inaugurated a new class instead, for managers of phone work, which I toured with.

This gave me some time to rethink my positioning. I reviewed the comments I had received, and I did what Zen practitioners speak of as using a "beginner's mind."

I think this example will show you the pluses and perils of product differentiation and positioning. I determined that The New Telemarketing™ was too adversarial. In my zeal to invent a better way to sell by phone, I adopted a rhetoric for promoting, and actually conducting the class, which was alienating.

In effect, I was saying: "My way is the best. Every other way is inferior."

This, folks, is a message that arouses defensiveness. And it's nearly impossible to sell to people whom we make defensive. They're too busy defending their wounded egos and planning counterattacks to even think of buying.

When you choose to be a consultant, you are claiming to

have superior know-how. If you were exactly as knowledgeable as your prospects, they'd be fools to hire you.

So the point needs to be made that prospects don't have the tools you have. But we have to communicate this idea without making them too uncomfortable. It takes very delicate positioning to do well.

We can't say, "Forget everything you've ever known about doing business. I have a better way!"

They'll think, "Hey, we've been pretty successful so far—in fact, successful enough to hire you, and you're telling us we're doing it all wrong?"

> You're good, but I can help you to be better.
> That's the message we need to get across.

Before I tell you how I'm curing the problem with The New Telemarketing™, I should point out some other data that suggested I might be unaligned with my market.

1. Sales of my best-selling book, *You Can Sell Anything By Telephone!* remained strong, year after year. Moreover, book readers who called me about my other products were still incredibly enthusiastic about the traditional telemarketing content that I had provided in that book.

No one said, "Gee, nice book, but I don't think those techniques would work, today." As a matter of fact, when I would try to persuade them that my ideas had evolved, and I had a better way, they seemed to feel I was repudiating something they liked!

2. Service bureaus, which do contract telemarketing, were growing fast, and they used traditional methods. If they were an utter disaster, such methods wouldn't persist.

So, struck by these developments, I had to revise my concepts. I determined that both methods could work, side by side. Indeed, it could be the case that person A might take to traditional selling just fine, while person B would need the new style.

Certain products and prospects might gravitate toward one or the other, as well! This thinking enabled me to have a product and a positioning breakthrough.

Instead of saying, "Don't sell that way!," I could be much more helpful by saying, "Here's exactly when you should sell that way, and here's when you should sell another way."

Philosophically, I had moved from a thesis (traditional telemarketing), to its antithesis (The New Telemarketing™), to a new synthesis:

Why not promote both?

Thus, a new course was born, Multi-Style Telemarketing™.

✳✳✳✳✳✳✳✳✳✳

I am going to reproduce my initial course description, to show you how I launched this program:

Multi-Style Telemarketing™
A Special One-Day Seminar with Dr. Gary S. Goodman

ONE SIZE DOESN'T FIT ALL...

So why should your telemarketing campaign sound like everyone else's?

To develop professional, winning telemarketing programs, you need to customize your approach.

Spray-and-pray methods offend elite prospects, and time-consuming conversational methods irritate fast decision makers.

Develop the style that's right for you, right for your product or service, and right for your customers.

In **Multi-Style Telemarketing™**, you'll hear several ways to open calls, describe products, close sales, and engineer commitment. You'll learn when and how to use traditional versus new telemarketing methods.

You'll learn to sell to all kinds of prospects: Cynics, Optimists, Realists, Sloths, Racehorses, Intellectuals,

Shoppers, Negotiators, Fence-Sitters, The Once-Burned & Twice Shy, and the Phone-Frightened.

You'll hear tapes of real sales calls—inbound and outbound. From $30 software upgrades to $1,000,000 investment sales.

And you'll gain practice in a supportive workshop setting, refining your own presentation. (Do you have a presentation? Bring it with you. You'll get a unique chance to polish it.)

You'll also learn:

New ways to handle secretarial screening—we'll get you through twice as often. Draft Call-Paths that are comfortable and compelling. Hear incoming service calls where reps upsell by 310 percent. Listen to customers taking the sale away from salespeople, making traditional closing unnecessary. Qualify prospects easily, while setting better appointments. Take the tension out of your calls, and put the fun and success back in.

YOU SHOULD ATTEND: If you're in telemarketing, inside or outside sales, if you set appointments, do order-entry or customer service, or if you manage people who sell, service, or persuade others by phone.

A SPECIAL INVITATION TO NONSALESPEOPLE and CUSTOMER SERVICE PERSONNEL: If you are being called upon to sell, but you don't feel comfortable, this is the seminar for you. You'll be able to devise a style that you can live with!

YOUR SEMINAR LEADER is <u>Dr. Gary S. Goodman</u>, veteran telemarketer, consultant, and best-selling au-

thor of nine books, including *You Can Sell Anything By Telephone!* and *Selling Skills for the Nonsalesperson.*

Here's What Participants Say About Gary Goodman's Telemarketing Programs:

"Much better than AT&T and Pacific Bell's programs." K.R., Leslie's Poolmart.

"Everything discussed was up-to-date and professional. I will recommend this seminar to everyone I know." H.B., American Express.

"Great ideas! Much better than what I'm currently using." D.S., Telemation.

"I enjoyed learning all the NEW ideas, moving away from the typical bombarding sales approach." B.L., USS Posco Industries.

"I really appreciate learning new material. I've been selling and servicing over the phone for ten years." J.L., Weitek Corporation.

"I will definitely recommend this seminar. It is going to make a big difference in my career." L.A., Allied Sysco.

West: May 9: Disneyland Hotel, Anaheim, California

Midwest: May 14: Chicago Hilton, O'Hare International Airport

East: May 16: Boston, Hyatt Regency Cambridge

Fee: $695 per person. EARLY BIRD DISCOUNT: Register by April 8 and pay only $595—save $100. TEAM SAVINGS: Send a team of four or more to the same seminar and save an additional $100 per person! Nonrefundable.

Seminar Agenda

8:45	Coffee, Seminar Check-In
9:00	Introduction, Overview, Participant Goals
	Why Prospects Resist Telemarketing Calls, and
	The Cure—Adapting Your Style, on the Spot
9:20	Building Credibility
9:50	Do's and Don'ts in Call Planning
10:10	Break
10:25	The First 30 Seconds: Getting Through Screening
	and Voice Mail
11:00	Anatomy of a Conventional Telemarketing Call:
	Outbound and Inbound Versions
11:45	Morning Questions
12:00	Luncheon
1:00	Preventing and Managing Objections
1:25	Consultative Telemarketing, Part 1
2:10	Break
2:25	Consultative Telemarketing, Part 2
2:45	Choosing the Right Style(s) for You
3:00	Scripting Workshop
3:40	Q & A; Troubleshooting
3:55	Evaluation
4:00	Adjournment

****

I'm really proud of myself for having made this adjustment. I feel I'm perfectly aligned with my market because I'm saying:

There are several ways to succeed in telemarketing.

This tells people what they want to hear. But it's also valid.

Market-Test Your Ideas

It makes sense to test your ideas before you roll them out.

Now, when I roll out a class, it costs several thousand dollars, months of time, and a major commitment of future resources. So I try to get some client input before deploying my assets.

What I did with the new course was simple. I called some people who had been to my management seminar and who had expressed interest in The New Telemarketing™. I faxed them the copy you just read, and, as it turns out, I got immediate and powerful positive feedback.

One client called back within twenty-four hours and committed to send four people to the Chicago site. They had to fly in, so the investment they made was many thousands of dollars when you tally the tuition, flight, hotel, and ground expenses.

This told me I had touched a nerve.

If you're a solo practitioner, or you run a small business, you have to be able to make good inferences from a few data points. You can't wait until all the facts are in before you make your move.

First, the facts are never all in. As Aristotle put it, human conduct occurs in a world of probabilities, and not certainties. If a class or a consulting product looks like it is going to be a winner, we need to jump on the opportunity.

Early in my consultancy, I inferred from my first Cal State, Los Angeles seminar that I was onto something. Within two weeks, I had returned to DePauw, where I burned up the phone wires promoting my class to other colleges. Within eighteen months, I had brought it to thirty-five universities, coast to coast.

I had been passively thinking of training other people in telephone skills since my early days at Time/Life. It was eight years from the time of the original thought until I ran that first college-sponsored class.

Sometimes the gestation period can be long, between conception and delivery of a consulting formula. That's fine. It's even better to do some research before you jump into the arena.

I waited until two fuel crises had made people mad about traveling everywhere to do business. They were ready to explore the phone as an alternative by the time I offered information about how to do it.

But when you're ready to move into your market, be prepared to do so with everything you have. You'll get there first, and you'll be distinguished for having done so.

How to Become a Consultant in twelve Weeks

Here's exactly what I would do to establish myself as a consultant in twelve weeks.

Week 1

Settle upon a business name. Are you going to use your own name? I started as Dr. Gary S. Goodman, Communication Consultant, before incorporating as Goodman Communications Corporation.

Most businesses in America utilize the founder's name in the title. This doesn't mean you have to, but you can, without feeling like an egomaniac. Hyatt, Hilton, and Marriott have done okay, as have all of the major consulting firms, such as Arthur Andersen and Ernst & Young.

Some people like to call themselves the Smith Group, as if there are more people at headquarters than one lonely pioneer. There is a belief that if you sound like a heavily populated company, people will perceive you with greater seriousness.

Use your own judgment. I'd avoid gimmicky names, such as You Can Count On Us, Consultants. It sounds like carpet cleaners.

Order letterhead and at least two phone lines. Don't use the same line for voice and fax transmissions. If you can afford it, you might consider getting a third line that you can dedicate to the making of outbound calls. That way, you don't have to switch back and forth.

Go to the library and come away with information about at least one hundred companies to target with your marketing efforts. Copy their listings from business directories, and note the names of at least two senior officers to whom you can address your letters and mail.

Write a cover letter announcing who you are and what you propose to contribute to your clients. Keep it short. I like to make my introductory letters a single page. Strangers will generally read one page, but they might discard two or more.

Compose a basic telephone script that emulates what you've said in your letter. Not in tone, but in text. Our calls should sound conversational and less formal than our letters. I would make the goal of your call the setting of an appointment.

Make as many calls as it takes to set up two appointments for the second week. You may have to go through your list of one hundred companies to open two doors. That's okay, because you're in a learning mode.

If you've done all of these things, you've done well for your first week! I'm proud of you!

Week 2

Go Back to the Library

Ask the reference librarian to show you the Standard Rate & Data Service volumes that list publications in your consulting field. For example, I focus upon many of sales and service newsletters and magazines.

Note their names, addresses, phone and fax numbers, and editors' names.

Also note the names of the business and events editors at local and regional newspapers. These will congeal into very valuable press lists for you.

Have a Business Head-And-Shoulders Photo Taken

Don't have Uncle Bob do it. You don't have to pop for a Richard Avedon portrait, but you should have a professional take it.

Try to smile. Look into the lens and think, "You can trust me—I'd never hurt you." No Cheshire grins, please.

Write a News Release That Announces Your New Consulting Practice

Remember to answer these questions: who, what, when, where, and why. Write the release in the third person. Here is an example:

For Immediate Release

Dr. Gary S. Goodman, of Glendale, CA, announces the formation of a new communication consulting firm, Goodman Communications Corporation.

GCC will offer public seminars and on-site employee training in the areas of telephone etiquette, customer service, and telemarketing.

Goodman is a former college professor at California State University, Northridge; the University of Southern California; and DePauw University.

Goodman says, "Companies are losing billions of dollars every year in lost productivity through wasteful telephone techniques." His solution is to reengineer calls so they are shorter, but better.

Goodman can be reached at: GCC, 631 West Broadway, Glendale, CA 91204. Phone: (818) 243-7338. Fax: (818) 956-2242.

Send the Release to Your Entire Press List

I like to fax my releases, because it adds urgency, saves time, and I can do it with a few keystrokes from my computer.

I'll mail releases and articles if I'm including a photograph.

I wouldn't expect to garner much exposure with your first release. You may not get any publications to run it.

But that doesn't matter, because you will have started the

process of propaganda that ultimately takes root in the minds of editors.

The more of you they see, the more important you'll become to them.

I'm continually amazed by how this works with my articles. As more of them get published, even more editors decide to publish them.

It's not quite a feeding frenzy, but it's my inference that the editors in a subject area are all looking at each other's publications, to keep up with the competition.

When they see my byline, or articles that I've been interviewed for, especially as the sole source of information on a topic, my stock soars.

Naturally, when they need a comment on a subject related to my expertise, they're going to turn to the source that has been feeding them stories and releases on a steady basis.

One publication mentioned my name, when readers called and asked its editors who they recommended as a consultant! That's a great reward for cultivating a relationship.

When you write on a regular basis, you can stockpile articles and send them out on a regular schedule. One editor, who is part of the Direct Marketing Association, asked me for an article.

He was on a tight deadline. Within five minutes, I faxed two articles, so he could choose the one he preferred. Because of my fast response, I made a friend, while encouraging that publication to seek my contributions in the future.

So get started building your relationship with the press. Feed them information on a steady basis.

And don't worry about rejection, or the fact that a large percentage of your submissions will be trashed. I hired an intern to whom I delegated the task of faxing one to two articles per week to about thirty publications.

At one point, she innocently asked, "Won't these editors feel we're bothering them if we send so much stuff?"

No way! It's their job to sift through it, and to judge its merit. It's ours, as consultants, to invest our time producing it.

Make Follow-Up Calls to Last Week's Contacts

I assume that you have kept adequate records of your first week's calls and fax and mail transmissions.

If you have been using a three-step marketing approach, such as (1) an initial call; (2) a mailer; and (3) a second call, it's time to enact Step 3.

You need to follow up on all of your mailers or faxes.

This is a sticking point for a lot of new consultants. The first two steps were pretty easy, weren't they? You made a first call to introduce yourself, and if the coast was clear, you asked for an appointment, then and there.

But, in most cases, prospects asked you to send them information. You bundled together your cover letter and any other materials you could insert, and sent the package off.

Now, four to seven days later, they should have received it and formed an impression of it.

You and I both know that a good number of the people who requested literature were duds. They did this to get you off the phone, because they're too timid to reject your effort outright.

So when you call them during Week 2, they'll play hide-and-seek with you. You'll seek, while they hide. This can be upsetting and frustrating unless we do two things.

One is an economy measure, and the other is an attitudinal adjustment. Before you send out any more mailers after speaking to prospects the first time, make sure to qualify them. Mention that you'll be pleased to mail or fax the material their way, and then ask:

> And if you like what you see, what will be the next step
> in developing a relationship?

Yes, this is similar to the line that I used when speaking to college administrators about sponsoring my seminars. When I teach this technique to salespeople, I call it:

The If-Then, Bottom-Line, Qualifying Question.

If a prospect gets unduly nervous when it's his turn to answer this probe, he's telling you he has no serious interest in buying, or perhaps no real authority to advance a relationship.

Your response should be polite. Conclude the call immediately with:

> Well, nice speaking with you. Good-bye!

In other words, jettison him immediately. You'll save yourself time, money, hassles, needless send-outs and faxes, unfounded hope, and a lot of hide-and-seek.

So Week 2 is a reality check, of sorts, on Week 1. When you make your follow-up calls, you'll sense who is worth pursuing, and who isn't.

Make More Cold Calls

I know, between doing the press release, and following up the first week's calls and literature, you're really busy.

But you still need to fuel your marketing engine. This means you should probably make at least fifty new contacts during Week 2.

Remember, because you'll be getting sharper in qualifying the interest of these people, you'll be sending out fewer packages. That curtails the number of follow-ups you'll need to make during Week 3.

So, you're busy, but you're also streamlining your process.

See the People, See the People, See the People . . .

When I was consulting for a former Marine turned entrepreneur, I was invited to watch him do some sales training before his new recruits.

He offered several pearls of wisdom. First, he stated that discipline "is the most important thing in life."

Then, he laid down his rules for selling. Rule #1 was simple:

> See the People, See the People, See the People . . .
> This was the fundamental rule for succeeding.

Frank made a big deal out of the fact that you didn't need to worry about being skilled in selling. In fact, you could be too clever.

Just demonstrate the product, and before you leave, make yourself do something crucial:

Ask for the order at least once.

Let's say you did a great demonstration, or you had a nifty chat, filled with rapport with the prospect. Then, you have earned the right to:

Ask for the order at least once.

Let's imagine a vastly different scenario. You were an utter bozo. Nothing worked as it should have. You mangled your words, and prospects seemed impatient to bring the curtain down on your act.

In that case, you should:

Still, ask for the order at least once.

This, my friend, is sage advice. You see, you should try to advance the relationship, no matter how well you think you've done in the selling process.

There are a few principles that I should share with you:

* Most prospects won't "close" themselves. They need to be nudged, and we're the nudgers.

* It is hard to read and interpret correctly the nonverbal communication between ourselves and prospects. They may invest us with high credibility because our act isn't slick and flawless. Or, we might not be doing as badly as we think. Public speakers, who suffer from stage fright, always think they're doing a worse job than the audience thinks.

* By asking for the yes, you get the prospect to tell you where you stand with respect to your presentation. If you're asking to move forward prematurely, you'll hear this, and you can back off.

One thing is for sure, as the Bible says:

Ask, and you shall receive.

I assure you that the more often you ask, the more often you'll receive!

During Week 2, I assume you'll meet with two prospects by appointment. Pat yourself on the back. This is a good start.

Week 3

Reflect, But Not Too Long

There is the story about the fellow who jumps from a high building, and about halfway to the ground, someone asks, "How you doing?"

"So far, so good!" he responds. I insert this story to say that it's hard to evaluate the effectiveness of a process when you're in the middle of it.

But, I think Week 3 is a good one to use to reflect upon your frenetic first two weeks in the consulting business. How did you do?

How many promising leads are you pursuing? Have you selected a good niche, when you think about the 150 prospects you called?

Are they expressing enough interest to encourage you, or should you move to another category of people to contact? If the feedback is strongly positive, you're into a good niche.

If it's indifferent or hostile, then it's time to go back to the library and look for another type of client to serve. The key to finding a good niche is to concentrate upon underserved market segments.

Ninety percent or more of the consulting services consumed in America are purchased by Fortune 1000 companies. So it would seem logical to serve that clientele if they're used to perceiving value in the use of consultants.

But what if this door is closed to you because you're just starting out, and you don't have a long list of achievements? It might be a good idea to find a category of business you can serve that doesn't erect such high entry barriers.

You could concentrate upon helping small businesses.

They're everywhere, in huge numbers. That's a plus, because you can find a ton of them close by. That makes them cheap to cultivate, because you can visit two to four every day, if you like.

There are few decision makers or decision influencers that you need to confer with. Usually, the president is the owner, and she can sign your contract without having to ask anyone else's permission.

Lists of small concerns are eminently available. The best, free list is the Yellow Pages. In fact, I suggest you use the Yellow Pages as well as Standard Industrial Classification codes to analyze what your target market should be.

How Is Your Pricing?

You've seen at least two prospects. Each one asked you how much you charge for your services.

When you mentioned the rate, did they seem pleased, nonplussed, concerned, or shocked? If they were pleased or nonplussed, your prices are low-to-reasonable in their minds.

When they grow concerned, or shocked, then your prices seem out of line.

Don't get me wrong. Your fees could be at the high end but also be a true bargain in terms of the value they represent. But client perception is important at this stage in your career.

You'll probably recall that my cassettes went from $14.95 to $199 within a short time. I had to start somewhere, so I started with what I thought was a reasonable price, given my rock-bottom cost of production.

My public seminars started at $25 to $35 per day, seventeen years ago. At the same margins, if we allowed for inflation, they would be $75 to $125 today. But, they're not . . . they're at $695.

I'm saying that you can always raise prices once you have obtained market acceptance at lower levels. A major task for you, during Week 3, is to figure out what it will take to get that first client, relative to the fees you're quoting, and the other strategies you're using in your marketing.

Send or Fax Thank-You Notes to the People You Met

It's a small gesture, but it makes a good impression. It shows respect for their time, and it's a chance for you to recommend taking the relationship to the next level.

You could suggest a second meeting, this time with the first contact's boss. Or, you could spread out in the firm in an effort to meet more key contacts who can support your program.

In some cases, your first meeting will result in a request for a proposal. If you feel you have enough data to write one that can succeed, go ahead.

If not, jump right back in with your prospect to ask for the information you need to know.

See the People You Made Appointments With During Week 2

You should be getting better at your cold calls, and you should have at least three to four appointments to see during Week 3.

Go Back to the Library, or to the Bookstore

It's time for you to inaugurate what continuing educators refer to as lifelong learning.

As I'm sure you can see, from having read this book, much of the work of a consultant doesn't take place on the clock, giving advice. It is devoted to earning the opportunity to give advice, on the clock.

This means it's in sales, marketing, and research.

During Week 3, I urge you to read three to four books on the subject of selling. I have written several that have reached best-seller status. And judging from the responses of the thousands of people who've called and written to me over the years, they'll help you.

Look for *You Can Sell Anything by Telephone!* and *Selling Skills for the Nonsalesperson.*

By the way, if you're new to selling, pick up anything that is on the shelf. You're bound to learn something from it.

You're also going to need motivation and inspiration. Personally, I like Robert M. Schuller's books. Pick up his work entitled, *Tough Times Never Last, But Tough People Do!*

In Week 3, you're probably doubting yourself. You might

feel a strong need for instant gratification, and for the sort of re-inforcement that tells you that you've made a smart career move.

That message may be running a little late, if you're waiting for it to come from the outside world. If it is, start developing a bedrock of faith that you will prevail. Reach out for the books and other materials that can give you new techniques and the desire to keep on, keeping on.

You might want to look for materials produced by the motivational speaker and writer, Les Brown. I have one of his videos that I watch while I'm on my exercise bike after I've concluded my business day.

Les has a theme that I encourage you to say during Week 3, and every week thereafter:

It's Possible!

It's possible for you to realize your dream of becoming a consultant. It's possible to struggle against difficult odds to win. It's possible that you might become the best consultant who ever entered this profession.

How to Stay Enthusiastic, Especially While You're Struggling

Some successful people have said that enthusiasm is the highest paid quality in the world.

As consultants, it is certainly one of our most precious possessions.

Nearly anything great can be accomplished with enthusiasm.
And little of any consequence is created without it.

How can we become enthusiastic, and more important, how can we stay that way?

Here are my ten tips for staying upbeat, positive, and in the winner's circle.

1. **Remember where you came from.** When I was growing up, I couldn't wait to get into the business world. To me, being

on my own, earning a paycheck was the greatest thing that could happen to anyone. What kid doesn't want a feeling of self-control and an unlimited cash flow? Well, I wanted it all, and when I started out, I was literally penniless. I worked as a bus-boy, a box boy, sold newspapers on corners, and my very first job out of high school was delivering FISH in a sweltering truck. Nonetheless, this enabled me to rent a one-room apartment and start working my way through college. A half-pound of ground beef, which I'd cook to perfection on my hot plate, was the picture of luxury and heaven to a still-growing eighteen-year-old. This is where I come from. And when I start to get down, I remember that kid and smile and think, "If this is how far I've come already, imagine where I can go!"

2. **Remember friends who didn't make it.** One of my best friends from grade school made a few wrong turns with his life and ended up gunned down by gangsters when he was just eighteen. At high school reunions we all still reminisce about Doug, and how wasted his life was. You never know when your time is up, even if you're a saint, so make years of enjoyment out of your days.

3. **No matter how low you get, remember, others have been lower still, and they've climbed out of their ruts.** Never give up on yourself, or your potential. Keep telling yourself good things about yourself, and all you've done to make the world better.

4. **You might be missing a small success ingredient, and if you keep plugging away, you'll find it.** I can't tell you how many times things have looked bleak for my consultancy, only to find that when things were darkest, a new beginning was waiting just around the corner.

5. **Make sure to make a profit from your loss.** Every setback contains valuable lessons. If you look at the lives of great achievers, you'll see a pattern of failure that precedes their successes. Some very rich people have gone broke several times before reaching a durable level of financial success.

6. **Take noble risks.** Try new strategies for solving old problems. Don't let yourself get complacent by trying not to lose. It's

impossible to avoid all risks, because life, itself, involves cease-less risks, many of which we're not consciously aware.

7. **Count your blessings.** We're so lucky to have bodies with parts that are in good working condition. Lots of people aren't as lucky as we are. Even temporary maladies can teach us lessons. When I was on the stump doing countless seminars, I'd often get laryngitis, which would force me to speak less. Sometimes I'd be lecturing with only a whisper and hand gestures. Each time this has happened, I've recovered with a sense of elation about my ability to communicate through the voice. How precious a gift this is! How often we waste words with petty comments. If we had a meter that restricted our daily allowance of words, we'd be a lot wiser in how we chose to use them, and we'd be much more grateful for this one of many basic gifts we enjoy.

8. **Do, right now, exactly what you fear.** Fear is like a bad partner in business, who is constantly wearing you down, wast-ing your emotional and financial assets. Fear keeps most of us from enjoying life and our jobs to the fullest. Are you afraid of public speaking? You know the antidote for that, don't you? Force yourself to speak to groups as often as you can. Through systematic desensitization, you can condition yourself right out of your fears. And the exciting thing is the fact that once you have witnessed yourself conquering a given phobia, your confi-dence will soar and you'll want to overcome others. Who knows, you just might become a daredevil!

9. **Innovate.** Do things differently. I'll take this suggestion, by the way, to extreme limits. For instance, when I'm in strange territory such as a new town, and I've rented a car, I don't mind getting a little lost. What do I mean by a little? Well, if I'm in the right zip code, I think meandering around is a good idea. You get to see new things and you get new ideas. Or I'll take a bus to get to a seminar site instead of taking a taxi or private car. Just the fact that I've shaken myself out of ordinary patterns helps me to see new things, and to see old things in new ways. That's what innovating is all about.

10. **Don't worry about feeling low, or getting periodically negative.** You could be priming yourself for some radical change of the good kind. Often, that sinking feeling or anger or disgust

with one's present circumstances will be just the incentive you need to get off the dime and change, for the better. Welcome the downs, so you can revel in the inevitable ups.

One of my all-time favorite movies is the classic *It's a Wonderful Life*, starring Jimmy Stewart. As you probably know, he plays a fellow who got down on himself so much that he was about to end it all. An angel rescued him by showing him what the world would have been like if he had never existed, and a sorry place it was. Stewart's character rebounded from gloom and celebrated his life, problems and all.

While there are many lessons in the movie, I think one stands out above all. No matter how gloomy things might seem, there is light breaking on the horizon. Hang in there long enough, and you'll see it.

Week 4

Start Keeping a Diary

By this point, you're experiencing a number of setbacks and rejections. You may not be used to them.

And I'm sure your friends, your mate, or your kids aren't, either.

While, if you're like me, you might want to share all of these ups and downs with someone, you can't. You'll jeopardize those relationships.

Other people, who haven't started a business or made a major change of careers, can't relate to what you're experiencing.

It doesn't matter that they love you and they wish you all the success in the world. They do.

But their capacity to empathize and to offer guidance is limited. They have their own hopes and challenges to confront. Being burdened with yours isn't necessarily what they signed up for.

Maybe you're not like me. You might be a great internalizer—you know, a person who would never wear his emotions on his sleeve. Like Mount Saint Helens, there could be in you a snowy surface that disguises a molten core, deep below.

Either way, I'm going to suggest you keep a diary. You can

make your daily entries in the morning or in the evening—it's all the same. But try to write at least a line a day that expresses your hopes and dreams, or mourns your disappointments and defeats.

Why do I recommend this? Because you're alone in your new pursuit, and it's helpful to have a nonjudgmental friend to whom you can pour out your true feelings.

That's your diary, pal. Believe me, it's not going to be put up for a Pulitzer, because it's not literature. That's not its purpose.

You don't have to check the spelling and grammar, and by all means, don't show it to anyone else. It's your private ruminations about the life of your business.

It will help you to let off steam. Spill your vitriol in its pages, and don't hold anything back. This way, you can get a handle on your real feelings, and start to cope with them.

I find that I can admit flaws that I wouldn't reveal in any other setting. That's healthy, because I can work on remedying them without having to mention to anyone what I'm working on.

You'll also start to see the kernels of new ideas. Sometimes, I'll be writing my thoughts down, and the title for a new book or seminar will pop into mind. I'll just put it into the margins, put a box around it, and move on.

Days, and sometimes months later, I'll scan my pages and take a fresh look at my little inspirations. The timing might be perfect to move on them, because my thinking and experience have evolved so I'm ready to act.

There's another benefit to having a diary: it's efficient. You can get something out of your mind or heart very directly. You don't have to set up an appointment with a pal or a therapist to emote.

You can open your notepad, or your laptop, and take care of business.

Start an Inspiration File

Speaking of writing, I strongly urge you to open a new file that is dedicated to inspiration.

This is the place to which you can turn on a daily basis to get your injection of motivation. My file is very eclectic, and that's okay, because inspiration can come from anywhere.

At one point, I inserted G. Gordon Liddy's line:

Whatever doesn't kill me, makes me stronger.

I found out through some later reading that he swiped it from Albert Camus, the great existentialist author. So what?

It's a great line, don't you think?

I like the line that I got from Les Brown:

It isn't over, until I win!

Mother Teresa is in there:

We can't do great things. We can do small things, with great love.

I'll even plant certain ideas so I can refer to them, later. One of these inserts starts with:

READ THIS WHEN YOU'RE FEELING DOWN

It goes on to remind me of all of the things I've accomplished against great odds. It finishes with:

YOU DID IT THEN
YOU'LL DO IT, AGAIN!

****

How Are Your Proposals Doing?

Let's look at the math of success.

By the end of the fourth week, you have probably made 250 cold calls. These, no doubt, resulted in ten to twelve appointments. (If they didn't, take a good look at my section on appointment setting in *You Can Sell Anything by Telephone!*)

You visited with the people, and you were invited to write four proposals. Five prospects weren't worth further attention, and three are in limbo. They might require more interaction before you determine whether they should be moved to the proposal stage.

So four prospects are in the pipeline. You have pending deals with them. How many should you close?

It's hard to say. We're hoping for one, but we probably won't know what we're going to get for another two to four weeks. I've found that the average time it takes to move from the first to the final stage of the buying process is six to sixteen weeks.

People aren't hiring a regular employee, so there isn't the urgency that induces them to say, "Gee, can you start on Monday?"

You're in an independent business, so they feel no obligation to begin your program at your convenience. I've found that traditional selling games that seek to accelerate decisions don't work too well in consulting.

"Hire me before someone else does!" isn't a very effective or credible appeal. So we need to be patient and wait it out.

This isn't to say that we're going to sit on our hands.

Your marketing machine should never be idle!

Just because you're waiting to hear from four prospects doesn't mean you should slacken in your promotional push.

Get more proposals into the pipeline!

Week 5

Reach Out to Other Consultants

This would be a good time to contact other small consulting firms to pick their brains.

I'd do some research to identify a handful of successful ones and then ask to see them. If you mention you're just starting out and you'd appreciate their input, you'd be amazed at how many will open their doors to you.

In some respects, you're in an ideal position to learn from experienced professionals.

You don't know enough to have a problematic ego!

When you're fresh to the field you can be sincerely nice and humble. Whatever you do, don't spoil this advantage!

People feel good about helping other people who ask for assistance, openly and without guile. If you're ever going to seem harmless, it's now.

So make the most of it. See the people who are successfully selling consulting contracts. Formulate five to ten critical questions that they won't mind answering.

* When you were just starting out, what did you find was the best way to get business? That seems innocent enough. It also gets someone to talk about his favorite subject: himself.

* What have you found to be a waste of time, when it comes to marketing?

* Who are the worst clients? And the best?

* If you had to start from scratch, today, what would you do first? Second? Third?

* Apart from what your firm specializes in, where do you see opportunities?

* What are the benefits in being in your kind of firm? The burdens?

* If I find an opportunity that's right for your firm, may I bring it to you?

* And will you be so kind as to do the same for me?

You can't help but learn if you ask these kinds of questions and you open up to the answers.

I was granted an interview with a prominent public relations advisor when I started my consulting practice. I saw his name in one of the Class Notes sections of my college alumni newspaper.

I wrote to him, congratulating him on his accomplishment that was referred to in the paper. I also mentioned that I wished to meet him when I came to his city. A few months later, I did.

Our meeting probably lasted thirty to forty minutes. He was cordial. I don't think I took from the encounter too many specifics about opening a professional office of one's own, but what did stick with me was his chutzpah.

He told me that he charged his clients about $10,000 per month, as a retainer. We talked about the psychology of retainers, and he explained to me how he could justify having several simultaneous retainers with various clients. I said it seemed to stretch him a little too thinly.

Well, I'm thinking about all of them, all of the time. Night and day!

I loved it. He was absolutely convinced that he was purveying top value. Because of his self-confidence, no client would dare to ask this gentleman to enumerate EXACTLY WHEN he was working on their account.

His response might be, "There's never a time when I'm NOT working on it."

Who could disprove it?

By visiting successful people, you'll debunk the myth most of us foster when we're new to a field that these survivors are gods.

They're usually bright, as well as crafty, but they're not superhuman.

That insight, alone, should be a great source of inspiration and help you to persist until you get enough accounts to make a living as a consultant.

Weeks 6–12

It may feel like you're the Bill Murray character in the movie *Groundhog Day*, but you should repeat, jot for jot, what you did during Weeks 1–5.

Even the press list stuff? Sure, double your press list. Send out another release or a new story. Get a reporter to do a human interest story about the pleasures and perils of starting your own small service business.

But, won't that make you seem pathetic?

If you're lucky. Even that could bring you business!

> You know the old adage that there's no such thing
> as bad publicity. It's true.

Just yesterday, I thanked the editor of a trade magazine for running my article on the topic of telemarketing turnover. It has resulted in about four inquiries so far. One of them has moved to a consulting proposal stage.

I said to him, "I think you may get some letters to the editor." Then, I added, "But I think they'll be favorable."

He replied:

"I don't care if they're hostile. You'd be amazed what we have to do to get reader reaction!"

Long after people forget your specific ideas, they'll remember your name. Politicians realize this. Becoming known to voters is their single, most important objective.

It takes several exposures to your name for it to sink into people's consciousness. So keep churning out the publicity!

Why Do Consultants Fail?

We've all seen the gloomy statistic that most businesses fail within the first three years. Some say the failure rate is as high as 90 percent.

Let's recall what that fellow once said was the major difference among consultants: it's marketing.

I believe you can be God's gift to clients, but if they don't discover you, you're going to join that sorry lot of business failures.

So forget about taking that extra degree at the university. You know, the one that, at least in your mind, will distinguish you from every other consultant.

Trust me when I tell you that it won't. I've earned five degrees: B.A., M.A., Ph.D., J.D., and the M.B.A. And I attended excellent schools.

Today, I face competition from people who haven't put their little toes into a college. Do I know more than they do? Absolutely.

Do my clients hire a better consultant when they choose me? Undoubtedly. But that's not the key issue:

Do clients always perceive great value in my credentials?

Not often enough. If they did, I'd be sitting with a huge share of the market, and degreeless advisors would all be twiddling their thumbs.

If I didn't have twenty-five years of solid, practical experience in my field, I doubt I'd earn much work at all. Because clients are ultimately buying results.

Prestige can help, but it doesn't pay the bills. Marketing does.

I've even disguised my degrees, on occasion, to get some consulting jobs.

Call it dumbing-down, to meet a client at his own level. I see it as an adjustment that is simply a part of appealing to your audience.

Consultants who fail are the ones who refuse to do this, or who ignore the market signals that say it's necessary to survive.

For instance, I have developed some very sophisticated and complex methods for improving telecommunications. I mean, this stuff is warp-speed compared to a parked car.

I'm so proud of it, I could burst. It is the result of true intellectual achievement. And, of course, it works.

But it's costly. Six-figure stuff, when it's implemented correctly. I only find about one or two clients at a time who have the coins and the motivation to move to this level with me.

Most of the action isn't soaring with the eagles, whether you're opening restaurants or dispensing advice. There are hundreds of McDonald's for every four-star restaurant you can find.

The action is crawling along with the turtles. Mass market stuff. In my field, that might translate into running courses in Telephone Etiquette for first-level secretaries and receptionists.

When I think about this, my ego feels that it has been impaled:

For THIS, I went to 15 years of college?

The short answer is yes.

That's the price we have to pay to remain financially viable as consultants. We have to meet the market at its own level.

We can't undershoot or overshoot it. We can't be too advanced or too far behind. This sort of calibration requires tremendous effort to effectuate.

And we have to lock up our egos to do it.

Fundamentally, consulting is a service business. Period.

We need to understand, despite our mammoth amount of training, experience, and expertise, that we are in the business of serving.

When you start to succeed, financially, you'll face your greatest challenges. You'll be tempted to believe your own publicity.

Occasionally, you'll have a solid win with a client. Your magic will really work, and you'll be exhilarated. You may even put away a good amount of money in the bank.

You'll be tempted to see your success as something that you can perpetuate with less and less effort. And you'll be dead wrong.

Success lags behind the effort that created it. When you start easing off, you're likely to persuade yourself that it was the relaxation that created the outcome. It wasn't.

The stonecutter needs to pound away at a surface one hundred times, before it will crack. The hundredth blow cuts through the rock's resistance. To the passerby, it was the lucky last blow that prevailed.

The stonecutter appreciates that it was the previous ninety-nine that set the stage for success.

When you're struggling, and almost unduly concerned about whether you're going to make it, you'll probably be just as conscientious and thorough as you need to be to sustain success.

Bill Gates, multibillionaire founder of Microsoft, put it well:

Your business will fail, he said, unless you're running scared all the time.

Welcome to one of the most exciting races you'll ever run.
I hope this book has been a good coach in showing you how to win in your sensational second career as a consultant!

Good Luck!

How to Craft Perfect Articles to Promote Your Consulting Practice

*G*ood public relations, and great publications, can mean the difference between having a struggling consulting practice and developing a multimillion-dollar career.

I would like to provide you with some extra information about how you should craft the articles you write for publication. This addendum will give you an experience in analyzing seven articles that I have published.

I'd like you to gain a better appreciation of what really brings in consulting business. So with that in mind, I would like to first brief you on what makes a perfect article. Then, you can read my articles and apply the critical criteria to them that I have supplied you with. Here are the questions that I'd like you to ask yourself as you review these pieces:

1. Can you guess which article brought me the most business and made the most money?

2. Which one caused the greatest controversy, made no money directly, but had a huge impact in developing my name in direct marketing?

3. Do the smarter, intellectual pieces sell more consulting than the nuts-and-bolts variety?

4. Which one was an utter dud, in every respect?

What constitutes the perfect article? There are four characteristics:

1. It gets published;
2. It's aimed at, and read by, the right people;
3. It positions you as an authority; and
4. It motivates the reader, your future consulting client, to call you immediately.

Let's examine these characteristics. First, what kinds of articles get published? At the top of the list are How-To offerings. For instance, I have a unit in my seminars that I call, How To Penetrate Secretarial Screening and Voice Mail.

It's very popular because it suggests an important problem that salespeople, and their managers, face every day. It also promises to tell them how to overcome it. Even this title could be improved if I made it more specific, which I should do when transforming it into an article.

"Five Ways to Penetrate Secretarial Screening and Voice Mail" will turn on editors who will either grab the article for immediate publication, or summarily toss it into the round file. There are additional ways to get the attention of editors.

One way is by becoming a contrarian. My article "Sometimes Dissatisfying the Customer Is Better" has been printed by numerous media, including *Time* magazine's Internet Web site, TimeVista. The title boldly disputes the customary maxims about customer satisfaction being the number-one goal of companies. I think it makes a serious point about how to engineer repeat business, and it has been well accepted by readers, as well.

I think it's important for a consultant to get the message across to potential clients that he or she sees things that are invisible to the rest of the world. Contrarian articles support that perception. They say, "Here is a smart person who doesn't always go along with the crowd."

Of course, you don't want to seem too far out from the sensibilities of clients. If you're too extreme, they'll be uncomfortable about bringing you in to help their organizations.

The perfect article is also aimed at the right people. This may be your toughest challenge. There is behavioral research that says that there is selective exposure to, and avoidance of, information. This means that the people who need your ideas the most will avoid many of the publications that they should be reading.

For instance, in the sales field, it's stunning how few sales managers and even vice presidents of sales and marketing read professional magazines and journals. You see, they often think they know how to sell, and that those media aren't right for them. They're too elementary.

So it may be wise to try to get your article on building sales in a magazine that they do read. That should be something like *Entrepreneur, Inc.,* or *Success,* instead of *Sales and Marketing Management.*

You should always appreciate that the people who need you aren't always the ones who will buy consulting services. They have to not see themselves as know-it-alls. I have a better chance of selling my services to a company president than I do to a vice president of sales, who may feel she's competing with me for credibility, and even compensation.

What do presidents read? It varies. A good place to reach them is through airline magazines. When they fly, like many executives, they may relax for a few minutes with an in-flight magazine. You can even try to get an article into a leisure publication. For instance, "How to Soft-Sell on the Links" may be something that a golfing magazine would run.

If honchos are introduced to you in a relaxed setting, or when they're pursuing leisure, their barriers are down, and you have a better chance of making a good impression with your piece.

Newspapers are worth publishing in because they have vast circulation, and there are no secretaries or other filters who will prevent your prospects from coming across your writing. The key to finding the right publications is in avoiding the coals-to-

Newcastle problem. Never try to sell to people who already feel they're more knowledgeable than you are. Go into publications where readers realize that they need help.

The third element that makes for a perfect article is that it positions you as an expert. I hate to say this, as a former college professor, but one of the tricks to building your credibility is to avoid quoting anyone else in your article.

Here's what I mean. Lots of aspiring consultants believe that they're going to make their stock rise by quoting people like Peter Drucker. Peter is, without question, like the Oracle of Delphi—brilliant and revered for it. I studied with him for two and a half years, so I respect his intellectual clout.

But he's famous enough, without my help. When I write articles, I avoid quoting anyone else unless I have interviewed them for the publication. That way, I sidestep competing with them for prestige. I seem like the fount of all knowledge on my subject, and implicitly, the reader is beguiled into believing that. If someone reads my work, they're more inclined to call me and not another consultant to whom I'm giving a free ride.

I don't plagiarize, let me make that clear. I publish my ideas, and not other people's. After all, I'm not writing scholarly articles, where a professor will mark me down if I don't use plenty of footnotes!

The trick in seeming like an expert is this: You don't want to come across as too haughty or too obtuse. Your ideas can't sound stiff and forbidding. Remember that credibility is mostly a matter of being likable, which means you need to seem 90 percent like the client, and 10 percent unlike them. The 10 percent of difference they seek, and will allow you, is in how informed about a specific topic you seem.

Should you showcase your college degrees in your article? I don't think it helps at all to have a byline that says:

by

Gary S. Goodman, B.A.

The Bachelor of Arts degree doesn't mean that much anymore, and other people who see you using it to establish credibility may even laugh at the attempt. An M.A. or an M.S. or an M.B.A. will confer more credibility, and there is some mileage to be gained from using them. I use my title, Dr., in my articles because it means more to the lay reader than putting Ph.D. after my name.

The final attribute of a perfect article is that it induces the right people to call you, immediately. Much of their motivation is informed by their perception of a need, and their evaluation of you as a source that they can draw upon to satisfy it. But whenever you can, make it easy for people to contact you. Put your phone number at the end of the article, if the publication will allow it. If not, make sure your company name and location are cited. This will make it easy for people to track you down.

Now, let's turn to these sample articles, and evaluate their effectiveness in aiding my consulting practice.

Employee Turnover: The Scourge of Telemarketing
by
Dr. Gary S. Goodman, 1995

Would a reportedly well-managed Fortune 1000 organization tolerate 400 percent employee turnover, especially if it meant having to hire, train, coach, counsel, compensate, and fire 1,200 people every year?

Well, there is a major metropolitan newspaper that does just this. And it's not alone. Countless companies, including telemarketing service bureaus, permit horrendous turnover in their telemarketing departments at staggering costs.

Estimates vary with respect to what companies lose by quickly turning over employees. United Parcel Service pegs it at $5,000 per person. A telemarketing recruiting organization says it runs approximately 25 percent of the annual salary and benefits of an employee.

Using the $5,000 figure, the newspaper is wasting about $6 million per year by having to fill and refill 300 positions. It could be handing each of the 300 people $20,000 bonuses every year simply for staying aboard!

Why does this waste persist, and what can we do to reduce it? To address telemarketing turnover adequately, we need to reengineer our model for staffing the telemarketing function.

Telemarketing managers suffer from a paradigm-lock that makes them think rampant turnover is a necessary and even desirable aspect of telemarketing. They probably developed their telemarketing skills in an atmosphere of high turnover, yet they survived. And in doing so, they have never stopped to question the fundamental belief that to build a telemarketing team you must have lots of losers for every winner who makes it. These same managers are probably proud of the fact that they could make it in what seems to be a survival-of-the-fittest atmosphere.

And so, like abusing parents who were the victims of abuse as children, telemarketing managers perpetuate the cycle of turnover without perceiving an alternative reality.

The first thing they need to realize is that incessant turnover isn't normal. It's unhealthy, and it needs to be cured. To improve, they have to step back and question the validity of their employee development routines.

What will a manager do if he believes that most of the people he's hiring are going to fail? Will he invest time and money in developing these individuals? Invariably, he won't. And his disinvestment philosophy will seem rational. After all, why throw good money away on people who won't be around tomorrow?

This results in a vicious circle of failure. The surest way to make someone fail is by leaving them alone to figure out how to do their job by themselves. Most people can't perform the abstract thinking necessary to develop a winning work routine. They need mentoring and very accurate feedback to be shown how to do a job, and some take more time to develop than others. If we tell them, "Sink or swim!" most will drown.

What we've failed to do is develop a proper methodology for helping the great majority of people to survive and thrive in telemarketing.

Some recruiters believe that they can succeed by hiring personality types. This is foolish. There is no single personality-based predictor of telemarketing success. Actors, debaters, and other extroverts are no more likely to succeed than the shy type you'll find over in the accounting department.

Many firms try to increase the odds of success by sticking a written presentation in front of people while demanding that they bring it to life. Most of these pitches are one-sided talkathons that customers reject. They're like dumb bombs in warfare. Dumb bombs miss more targets than they hit. So, blanket bombing is resorted to, just to assure minimal success. And blanket bombing disturbs everyone, including telemarketers who are shot down by hostile prospects.

The answer to solving the turnover problem isn't in doing more of what we're used to doing. This would be like using a leaking bucket to carry water from a lake to a campsite. Simply scampering faster with the same buckets won't solve the fundamental problem of water loss.

To do that, you need new buckets. Or, you need to move your campsite so it's closer to the lake. Or even better, you could consider building a pipeline that'll bring you water upon demand without wasting a drop.

In other words, only reengineering will reduce turnover in telemarketing. This requires us to change a number of processes and assumptions. In our consulting work we've developed what we call The New Telemarketing. It reduces turnover through the following principles:

1. We have to pay telemarketers a living wage that's commensurate with field sales compensation. Mainstream people require mainstream pay. If you try to underpay, you'll only attract marginal and transitional people.

2. Telemarketing should be full-time and not part-time work. Full-time work arouses a full-time commitment from managers and employees. People have enough time invested in the job to grow and develop. And they should receive full-time benefits, including health care coverage.

3. Straight-commission compensation should be avoided, unless it is willingly negotiated by manager and employee. Most people feel they aren't really employed unless they receive some pay for their efforts, even if they don't make sales.

4. A conversational form of telemarketing should be emphasized. This is less stressful for buyers and sellers. It's also more likely to be needs-based, to sound professional, and to succeed.

5. Telemarketers should have full account responsibility. If they've opened a new account through a cold call, they should service the account and resell it in the future. This gives them an incentive to stay in the good graces of customers and to stick around for reorders.

6. Significant resources should be invested in recruiting, training, coaching, and fully developing the capabilities of each person who is hired. In our consulting practice, we advise clients that they can expect to invest $2,500 to $3,500 per position to properly re-engineer their telemarketing program.

Rampant turnover can be cured. But it has to be treated properly and thoroughly.

****

What did you think of that one? I liked writing it, because I felt, and still feel, for that matter, that turnover is a scourge. This was widely published, and it appeared in *Teleprofessional* magazine, which is read by tens of thousands of managers in the tele-marketing field.

It was published as an editorial, and it appeared in the back of the publication. I received many calls from telemarketing reps who were thrilled that I seemed to be lobbying for raising their wages. But their managers didn't buy any services from me. I did sell a few audio seminars, however, to people who mailed in a bounce-back card that the magazine inserted.

Where I stepped on toes with this article was in insisting that curing turnover required elevating wages to meet those of field salespeople. That's not what the people-who-would-hire-me wanted to hear. They see telemarketing as a cost-cutting choice, so a messenger who says that costs must rise is shot.

Bottom line: not a good article for building one's practice.

✳✳✳✳✳✳✳✳✳✳

Ten Requirements for Measuring Telephone Effectiveness
by
Dr. Gary S. Goodman, 1995

Phone work is important to every successful orga-nization. Yet one of the areas that has been underde-veloped in recent years has been the measurement of telephone effectiveness.

Most modern phone centers, which are technolog-ically sophisticated, are still very primitive in their communication measurement techniques.

Certainly, they have machine-derived data about a rep's telephone time on and off calls, as well as aver-age call length. But they have very unreliable informa-tion about a given rep's telephone effectiveness, or communicative quality.

The typical approach to assessing call quality is the use of checklists by supervisors. These lists are usually concerned with whether a rep said something. This kind of presence-or-absence determination is one

of the most superficial ways of measuring any phenomenon.

Imagine watching your television news and hearing the meteorologist declare, "Yes, we had weather
today!" Of course, we had weather, but what kind of
weather was it, how does it compare to yesterday's,
and what is the prediction for tomorrow?

To get this kind of quantitative and qualitative report requires precise language and a meaningful use of
mathematics. To say, "It rained today" doesn't tell us
whether the rain was normal, above average, or below
average. Tell us it rained four inches today, and we
have knowledge that is much more meaningful.

This analogy illustrates two of the requirements
for measuring phone work. We need:

1. Clear categories and

2. Quantification of data to make it meaningful.

There are several other criteria that phone measures need to live up to, in order to be meaningful and
to improve telephone performance and customer outcomes.

3. Telephone communication categories need to be
operationally defined. For instance, in defining articulation, we don't say it is "being understandable to listeners." We define it as "the full-formation of words,
so they are immediately comprehensible to a listener
of reasonable sensibilities." This tells phone reps to
form words fully—in other words, it prescribes a
course of behavior that they can follow.

4. The categories need to be **exhaustive**. All meaningful events in conversations must be captured by
our measures.

5. Each category must be **isomorphic**. Categories
need to mean one thing, and only one thing, and not
usurp another category's territory.

6. They need to be **flexible**, to allow for unusual telephone events.

7. They need to **seem fair** to phone workers.

8. The measures need to create **inter-judge reliability**. They need to be usable by different managers with different experiential and educational backgrounds. These managers need to score the same conversations within a margin of difference of no more than 2 percent.

9. They need to be **tested and proven** across companies and across industries.

10. They need to relate to customer values and **improve customer sales and satisfaction** with greater reliability than the systems they replace.

We have been using a tool we developed for measuring phone work that we call TEAMeasures, which abbreviates Telephone Effectiveness Assessment Measures. This method meets these requirements and it has created tremendous results where it has been implemented. To date, approximately five million phone calls have been governed by the TEAMeasures method.

Our experience shows that managers can be so occupied with their present measurement method that they fail to stop long enough to compare it to other tools that are much more successful. To make the TEAMeasures system accessible, we're doing a series of seminars across the country called Monitoring, Measuring, and Managing Phone Work. For more information, please call 1-800-451-TELL.

Dr. Gary S. Goodman is an author and consultant as well as president of Goodman Communications and the Telephone Effectiveness Institute, in Glendale, CA. He is touring the country with his new seminar, Monitoring, Measuring, and Managing Phone Work. For information, please call 1-800-451-TELL.

****

This is the most intellectual article that I have published as a consultant. It is groundbreaking because, apart from my TEAMeasures™, there are very poor means of measuring the quality of calls.

What do you think this article brought me? I received a number of calls from trainers and human resources people who wanted a copy of my TEAMeasures™, for free.

I use this article as a reprint when I send out proposals. It certifies my techniques as being unique and fully thought-through. So, indirectly, the articles pays off nicely, but as a tool to make the phone ring with paying clients, it was a dud.

Frank's Five Pearls of Sales Wisdom
by
Dr. Gary S. Goodman, 1995

While I was doing a telemarketing consulting project a while back, I decided to sit in on a sales training session that was being taught to new salespeople by the owner of an office machine distributorship.

There weren't any fireworks that came from his style. But there were some pearls of wisdom that came from this ex-Marine, turned entrepreneur, that are worth repeating. Here are five of Frank's best tips for any salesperson:

1. Selling is so easy, it's hard. The work is very straightforward. You talk to people and give them good reasons for buying what you have. We make it difficult by thinking there's more to it than this.

2. The three rules of selling are: See the people; see the people; see the people. It's a numbers game, so see more folks and you'll close more deals. (The same tip applies directly to phone work, as well.)

3. Cold calling is the only reliable way of growing your client base. Don't wait for them to come to you—go to them.

4. Don't try to see people who don't want to see you. If they duck your calls or visits, cross them off your list. There are so many people who will be happy to talk with you that you're wasting precious time with those who don't want to.

5. Don't allow yourself to get too smart. Oldtimers get into slumps because they forget to do the basics. Newcomers to sales outsell many veterans because they do exactly what they're told. They don't have enough experience to doubt what they're hearing from their managers and trainers. So they do the basics, and they succeed. That is, as long as they stay green.

Frank philosophized a little about the meaning of life, but even this foray into potential abstraction was anchored to reality. He said: Discipline is the most important thing in life.

Getting yourself to do what you don't want to do, but what has to be done. That's what separates winners from losers.

Frank had a few salty aphorisms that can't be restated here. They were also succinct, and right on point.

You'd expect no less from a Marine.

****

From the sublime to the simple, right? I don't think I've written a simpler piece than "Frank's Five Pearls." This one is truly appreciated by sales managers because it tells them nothing new!

It has brought me more invitations to do speeches and seminars at sales meetings than any other piece I've reproduced here. How come?

It isn't threatening. In fact, it reinforces what sales managers have been preaching since time began. That's why they love it. It isn't me, or about me. IT'S THEM!

✱✱✱✱✱✱✱✱✱✱

The Fastest Way to Free Internet Phone Calls
by
Dr. Gary S. Goodman, 1996

Within five minutes, you're going to be able to make free long-distance phone calls through the Internet.

I'm not going to slip you a bootlegged version of some developer's software. Nor am I going to force you to withstand the quirky quality that current Webphone connections make you suffer through as calls are bounced across satellites.

You'll be able make free calls with your current Web browser while enjoying the fidelity of your everyday long-distance carrier. How can you pull off this minor miracle?

Go to AT&T's free 800 phone directory on the Web (http://www.tollfree.att.net/dir800/). This site lists nearly every company that has a published, toll-free number with that carrier.

Of course, you'll be able to look up numbers, one at a time, and call them for free. But there isn't much leverage in that.

AT&T's site enables you to do something else that can save you a bunch of money. You can search by category, as well. So if you're trying to build a list of chiropractors, or security services, all you need to do is type those descriptors in, and you'll see a beautiful display of free numbers across America.

For instance, I searched for software companies because I wanted to sell them my telemarketing audio seminars. Within seconds, a list of over 2,000 names of companies, along with their locations, as well as their free 800 numbers scrolled down my screen.

With a quick point and select manipulation, I copied the list into a word processing file, where I saved it and did a little text manipulation.

In minutes, I was calling through the list without spending a penny for phone calls!

AT&T's Internet site helped me to negate two major costs of telemarketing: list acquisition and phone costs. Add to these benefits the fact that I'm saving time by developing and quickly testing a list, and you can appreciate how powerful a tool this is.

By knocking down the cost of telemarketing by six to eight dollars per hour, simply by making calls free, I can pass those savings along to employees in the form of higher wages and commissions. That'll help me to attract and retain better people, and improve my productivity even further.

Making 800 calls will have some other interesting impacts. You'll frequently reach the customer service department instead of a grumpy receptionist or a cold machine, as you would by calling a company's regular number.

These paid-to-be-cheery folks will disclose nearly anything you want to know, about who-handles-what in the firm. They'll connect you with them, and your prospects will be more likely to answer the phone because they'll hear an internal ringing of the phone, instead of an outside ring.

The point is, you'll be screened out less often. That'll result in more completed presentations, and more sales.

I have to say that AT&T's free directory has made me a more effective communicator.

I feel a special sense of patience with prospects now, knowing that it's their dime that I'm investing!

****

Yes, I have my radical days, and it was during one of these that I crafted the Free Internet Calls piece. You probably guessed that this has been my most controversial article. It says, "Use someone's toll-free number to sell him something."

This appeared in *Direct Marketing News* and at their Website. It elicited frothy letters to the editor, asserting that I was unethical and a generally bad guy. Well, this seems like an utter failure, right?

It wasn't. I created an incredible buzz in the direct marketing community, and my name was on the lips of more people than ever before. I received calls of support, and suddenly I was getting referrals from marketing companies that I had never been acquainted with before.

You know the old aphorism that there's no such thing as bad publicity, don't you? It is true. Not only did the article create a sensation, but the letters to the editor gave me secondary publicity, as well.

****

Build Your Own Free Lists with the Web
by
Dr. Gary S. Goodman, 1996

Enthusiasts say the World Wide Web is a great economic leveler.

Small companies and individuals can compete with the biggies and use their creativity to attract attention as a substitute for spending big bucks through conventional advertising.

Well, there's another way that the Web can help the financially challenged or the just plain thrifty. It is in developing a free marketing database. Lists are in abundant supply if you know where to look and you use a little creativity to leverage different Web sites.

Why go into cyberspace for a list? Getting lists from brokers can be inconvenient and costly, especially if you're telemarketing. When I go through conventional list sources, I usually have to buy a minimum of 5,000 names. That'll set me back $500 to $1,000, and I'll have to wait a week or two for delivery.

I don't need 5,000 files to make an inference about the viability of a category. I may need only dozens or hundreds of names, addresses, and phone numbers that are geographically concentrated or dispersed.

You can currently go to various free Web sites and download as many basic data files as you want within minutes.

Some sites are intended for job seekers. They'll have as many as 100,000 companies in their databases. The **Nationjob Network** is an example. (See: http://www.nationjob.com/.)

One of my favorite free database sites is **Switchboard,** which contains 10 million companies. (See: http://switchboard.com/.) You can search by company name and by geographical location.

For instance, I wanted to develop a list of high-tech firms, so I entered the partial word, "technolog." This brought up about a thousand firms with technology or technologies in their names.

I got the same result with the word "system." If you want investment companies or mutual funds, try "investment" or "fund." And if you want to develop a quick list of a stock brokerage's nationwide branches, type in "Smith Barney" or "Merrill Lynch."

Within seconds, you'll be rewarded with a list that you can either download directly or copy into a word processing or database application.

One of the benefits of testing lists this way is the fact that it's private. You don't have to bare your soul to a list broker who could be passing on your marketing moves to competitors. Frankly, I prefer to do my systematic failing, i.e., list testing, in private.

And there's a time to use conventional list sources. It's <u>after</u> you've done the preliminary work with free database services that are there in the ether, waiting for you to use, night or day.

✶✶✶✶✶✶✶✶✶✶

I gored the ox of the database publishing industry with the Free Web Lists article, but my clients and readers loved me for it. Immediately, they started saving thousands of dollars on their list acquisitions.

I'm proud of this one, because I broke the story on finding and using the Internet resources in this manner. This established me as an author in the Web marketing field, and it wowed lots of people. Its economic value has been tremendous to me.

✶✶✶✶✶✶✶✶✶✶

Save Time and Cut Sales Costs by Reducing Undeserved Follow-Ups
by
Dr. Gary S. Goodman

How often have you invested precious hours following up with certain prospects, only to find that there was no real buying interest?

It seems to be an occupational hazard—following up with people who don't deserve an ounce of additional sales attention.

What irks salespeople is the fact that many of these prospects realize at some point early in our process with them that they're not worth our continuing attention. Yet, salespeople are the last souls they let in on the secret.

Prospects of this type may be embarrassed to tell the truth, or they may feel that an outright rejection is something we can't handle. But ask a veteran salesperson what she prefers—to be led along a never-ending trail, or to be told, flat-out that there's no hope in sight for a sale. She'll say she prefers a harsh reality over a fool's paradise.

How much does useless follow-up work cost vendors, and, ultimately, our customers? We've calculated that for every casual inquiry or prospect who is sent a brochure or a fax, approximately two hours are wasted in follow-through activities. This could mean hundreds of wasted dollars each time.

It takes about an hour for the average company to enter the prospect's name into a database, to package a brochure and a cover letter, and to ship them. It takes about fifteen minutes each time a phone call is made to follow up the mailer. And the average seller will make four or five calls to pursue a literature request.

There are also a lot of hidden time-wasters, such as the thinking time that a seller and his manager might invest in hoping that the lifeless prospect will become a great customer. Add to this the paranoia time that is invested when sellers worry that their competitors are getting the deal that they seemed to miss, and you have a huge misapplication of organizational resources.

What can we do to spare ourselves some of this wasted effort and added expense? Here are a few tips:

1. At the time someone requests literature, or you suggest it, add a hook to it by asking, "And if you like what you see, what'll be the next step?" If they're fuzzy in responding, they're probably not worth any follow-up, and you may be ill-advised to even send out the piece.

2. You should feel free to negotiate the communication rules between yourself, as a salesperson, and the prospect. Ask prospects to tell you, explicitly, if and when they are no longer interested in your attention. For instance, you can say this:

"We normally pay a lot of attention to people who show interest in us, as you've done. This is very costly, but it's worth it. If there comes a time when you don't feel there's any point to our efforts with you, please say so, and you'll save us both a lot of time, okay?"

3. If you've already invested time in developing a prospect, and they don't seem to return your calls, fax them a note requesting clarity as to where you stand. I say the following:

"If your firm is truly interested in moving forward with our program, please let us know. If not, we would be most grateful if you could share a few words with us as to how we may have missed the mark in developing a productive business relationship with you. In the space below, please share your thoughts by fax. Thank you very much."

It's nearly impossible to improve as salespeople unless we obtain quality feedback from customers at vital points in our relationship. It's up to us to ask for feedback and to explain to prospects that they can help us to keep selling and buying costs down.

Dr. Gary S. Goodman is an author and consultant as well as president of Goodman Communications and the Telephone Effectiveness Institute, in Glendale, CA. He is touring the country with his new seminar, Monitoring, Measuring, and Managing Phone Work. For information, please call: 1-800-451-TELL.

✳✳✳✳✳✳✳✳✳✳

This article has been useful to show vice presidents of sales how their salespeople waste time. It isn't threatening, and it makes a good reprint.

Telemarketing: Factories Without Roses
by
Dr. Gary S. Goodman, 1996

Rosie the Riveter was glorified during World War II. She held down a factory job while men went off to fight for the American Way.

Fifty years later, her granddaughter might be working in a factory as well. She punches a clock, earns an hourly wage, has a strict quota of units to produce per hour, and is closely supervised.

But she doesn't assemble airplanes or tanks. She isn't the darling of American society, made into a poster girl. If anything, she has low status and if she reveals her occupation to strangers, they'll wince.

She is today's factory worker—the telemarketer.

Hundreds of thousands of people make and take phone calls for a living in centers that can cover acres of land. Where farms once were, there are now massive, computer-driven phone-factories that employ students, retirees, moonlighters, Moms and Dads, and nearly anyone who can read from a written script.

Typical of today's phone factories is APAC Teleservices, with locations throughout Iowa. It has approximately 7,000 people on the phones, setting appointments, performing surveys, and even taking customer service calls for United Parcel Service.

APAC has benefited mightily from the corporate trend of outsourcing. Recently having gone public, it boasts a stock price with earnings multiples characteristic only of high-technology companies. During a recent sell-off in the broad stock market that lowered share prices of favorites such as Disney and McDonald's, APAC's stock actually rose.

Clearly, Wall Street thinks the telemarketing factory is the business of the future, but is it? Can it escape from the woes that have afflicted previous factories, whose products consisted of plastic and steel? Can it avoid the labor problems that have presented themselves in the past?

Although the telemarketing factory is a relatively new phenomenon, born out of improvements in software and telephone technologies, it is already facing formidable challenges. One problem is employee retention.

Typically, telemarketing centers experience 400 to 1,200 percent annual turnover among phone workers.

A major metropolitan newspaper that operates an in-house circulation sales group of 300 must hire 1,200 people per year to keep its phone chairs filled.

This means it is turning over its entire sales force every ninety days. At an estimated cost of $5,000 per lost rep, the company is spending $6 million annually to recruit, train, coach, compensate, and lose its staff.

Professional telemarketing service bureaus fare no better. Why can't the industry retain its frontline people? Several factors contribute to the turnover problem:

1. Compensation. Telemarketing jobs are usually benchmarked against clerical, and not sales, positions. This means that they more frequently pay minimum wage than a skilled-labor rate. Full-time telemarketers earn between $13,000 and $20,000 per year. Field salespeople usually earn $25,000 to $50,000 per year.

2. Bad reputation. Headlines about telemarketing scams and hostile legislation have had their impact on the psyche of workers.

3. Poor management. Most telemarketing managers have risen through the ranks, having been successful on the phones. They have little formal education in management, and as a group, they tend to shun continuing education classes.

4. Few career tracks. Most people perceive phone work as a dead-end job, without futurity. First-line supervision jobs are few, and that work is largely dedicated to policing compliance with scripts. Thus, it isn't attractive.

5. The work itself. Telemarketing work is designed to be robotic and repetitious. Managers believe that the best telemarketers will repeat the same presentations, the same way, throughout a working shift. They discourage creativity and communicative innovation.

People with intelligence and ambition tend to be alienated from such environments. As in factories, technologies such as predictive dialers that can queue up prospects for telemarketers to speak to are used to speed up the assembly line. Increasing amounts of productivity are expected from workers, without promise of additional compensation.

If telemarketing centers are factories, what's missing from the picture?

Unions. In most cases, unions haven't been able to penetrate call centers. And it isn't for a lack of trying.

According to the president of a local of the Communication Workers of America, when they try to organize workers, telemarketing firms flee across state lines to set up shop in anti-union environments.

If unions do score some major victories, it is likely that telemarketing will follow the lead of other types of factories. It will move its work offshore.

There is already a robust telemarketing industry in western Europe, but its cost structure isn't much more attractive than that to be found in the United States. Word has it that our phone jobs will be shipped to India.

With high unemployment, cheap land, plummeting international long-distance costs, and hundreds of millions of English speakers, that country could become to telemarketing what Mexico is becoming to television sets.

Why worry about pleasing Rosie when Rosa will be grateful to work for a dollar a day?

Dr. Gary S. Goodman is the publisher of the Sales and Service Newsletter and Executive Director of the Telephone Effectiveness Institute, in Glendale, CA. Between August and November, he'll be touring twelve cities with his new seminar, Eliminating Telemarketing Turnover.

∗∗∗∗∗∗∗∗∗∗

This is a big-picture article. It made a number of CEOs call me and treat me as a peer. It also helped me to add a new component to my consulting practice, as a manager of outsourced telemarketing programs.

I encourage you to write articles on a regular basis. Transform your consulting experiences and insights into additional cash, in this manner. Moreover, you'll feel proud of the fact that you're an author, and that your ideas are definitely fit to print!

— GSG

Afterword

I truly enjoyed writing this book, and I hope you got a lot out of it, as well. Consulting is exhilarating, but it can also be difficult and lonely.

If you want to share your war stories with me, or you have any questions, please let me know. As you know, I have products and services that can make your consulting career more productive. After all, I am also a consultant's consultant. So please stay in touch!

Dr. Gary S. Goodman
P.O. Box 9733
Glendale, California 91226
(818) 244-8355, (818) 243-7338
Fax: (818) 956-2242
e-mail: salesdoc@earthlink.net

Index

publicity, *(continued)*
    articles as, 40–44
    books as, 48–49
    campaigns, *see* campaigns,
        publicity
    and making predictions, 38–39
    manufacturing news for, 38
    news releases as, 39–40
    public seminars as, 98–99
public seminars, 97–100

reengineering, 2
rejection, taking, 57–58
repositioning, 117–120
reprints, article, 44
risks, taking, 136–137
routine, consulting, 91–95
    customizing step in, 93
    first-level one-on-one
        coaching in, 93–94
    first-level seminars in, 93
    management-level seminars
        in, 94
    management one-on-one
        coaching in, 94
    needs assessment in, 92
    periodic enhancements of,
        94–95
    written proposal for, 92–93

salary, *see* compensation
sales letters, 71–84
    as alternative to phone calls,
        71–73
    avoiding stiffness in, 72
    brochures vs., 84
    indirect selling in, 82
    length of, 81–82
    openers in, 73–74
    packet with, 72
    sample of, 75–81
    testimonials in, 82–84
    "you" in, 72–73

Schuller, Robert, on big projects,
    96
selling
    face-to-face, 69–71
    by letter, 71–84
    marketing vs., 51
    by phone, 56–67
seminars
    first-level, 93
    management, 94
    public, 97–100
SICs, *see* Standard Industrial
    Classification codes
slow periods, handling, 3–5
social recognition, consulting
    and, 28
special skills, consultants', 20–21
specialty media, publicity in,
    46–47
Standard Industrial Classification
    codes (SICs), 55
success, visualizing, 58–59,
    70–71
systematic desensitization, 58

Telephone Effectiveness
    Assessment Measures
    (TEAMeasures), 85–86
telephone lines, 125
telephone(s)
    cellular, 116
    overcoming fear of, 58–59
    setting appointments by, 67–68
    see also telephone sales
telephone sales, 56–67
    avoiding waste in, 66–67
    importance of discipline in,
        57–58
    and phone-fear, 58–59
    sample talk for, 60–67
    selecting time for, 56
    and taking rejection, 57–58